D1382746

Moral Philosophy
and the
Modern World

Moral Philosophy
and the
Modern World

DONALD PHILLIP VERENE

CASCADE *Books* · Eugene, Oregon

MORAL PHILOSOPHY AND THE MODERN WORLD

Copyright © 2013 Donald Phillip Verene. All rights reserved. Except for brief quotations in critical publications or reviews, no part of this book may be reproduced in any manner without prior written permission from the publisher. Write: Permissions. Wipf and Stock Publishers, 199 W. 8th Ave., Suite 3, Eugene, OR 97401.

Cascade Books
An Imprint of Wipf and Stock Publishers
199 W. 8th Ave., Suite 3
Eugene, OR 97401

www.wipfandstock.com

ISBN 13: 978-1-62032-689-3

Cataloguing-in-Publication Data

Verene, Donald Phillip, 1937–

　　Moral philosophy and the modern world / Donald Phillip Verene.

　　xiv + 148 p. ; 23 cm. Includes bibliographical references and index.

　　ISBN 13: 978-1-62032-689-3

　　1. Ethics, Modern. I. Title.

BJ41 .V46 2013

Manufactured in the U.S.A.

In memory of
Marco Olivetti
1943–2006
Friend and colleague of many years
Professor of the Philosophy of Religion
University of Rome "La Sapienza"

Finally, they chased the gods out in order to live in the temples themselves.

—Jean-Jacques Rousseau

Contents

Preface

THERE IS AN OLD principle in philosophy that to say what something is, say what it is and say what it is not. The two parts of this book follow this principle. The first part intends to revive the role of prudence in moral philosophy. The second part points to forms of conduct in the modern world that lie outside the moral but must be taken into account in order to understand the moral: the ideological selfhood of the terrorist; the psycho-sociopath, who, born without conscience, is puzzled by moral motivation in others; and the technologically oriented person, who is progressively unable to choose while believing that technology increases the possibilities of choice. I have considered these forms of conduct in various ways over a number of years. I bring them forward here as aspects of a general moral theory.

Ethical discourse in the modern world has lost its ability to speak about the good, virtue, the formation of character, and the good life. Modern ethics is dominated by a quest for the certainty of a decision procedure that will allow the individual facing a problematic situation to make a moral choice. Such choice may be guided by the practical reason of the categorical imperative—to act such that the action could become a universal law—or it may seek a solution by attending to utility—to what would produce the greatest good for the greatest number. The variations on these two themes of moral decision have culminated, in the past few decades, in the pursuit of applied ethics.

The sun never sets on the vast world of applied ethics, which stretches from agricultural and business ethics, through medical and military ethics, to the moral issues of YouTube and the ethics of zoo management. Applied ethics is a self-enclosed world of academic institutes, centers, conferences, and journals, held together by one common method: the argument of pro and con. All factors and evidence of a particular issue must be adduced, both sides of the question assessed, and then a possible solution advanced.

The drama is played out over and over, with variations only in subject matter. Since it is not beyond human wit to discover a counterargument for any argument advanced, the antinomic world of the applied ethicist is what Hegel called a "bad infinity," a series in which one more step beyond the last can always be taken.

When applied ethics was only beginning to take full shape as a field, Alasdair MacIntyre published an article titled "Does Applied Ethics Rest on a Mistake?" (*Monist* 1984). He took his title from the well-known essay of H. A. Prichard, "Does Moral Philosophy Rest on a Mistake?" (*Mind* 1912). Prichard's concern was that it had become unclear what books on moral philosophy were trying to show, and, when their aim was clear, why they were so unconvincing and artificial. MacIntyre's point was that it is a mistake to hold that ethics is a theoretical pursuit that can in some fashion be applied toward the solution of particular problems, in the way that scientific theory can be applied. Moreover, MacIntyre's view indicates that applied ethics is dangerous because it leads to the belief that ethics has a technical aspect, that it can become a problem-solving activity, resolving human problems by pro or con investigations when in fact applied ethics is a completely artificial enterprise. When thought leads us to believe that the human condition can be grasped and its paradoxes resolved, simply by the application of argument to issues, we subscribe to a kind of rational madness from which there is no exit—going from one argument to another. Overcome with argument, philosophy has forgotten its original purpose: the search for human wisdom and the self-knowledge that typifies it. To eschew the ability of argument to resolve the real issues of human life is not to abandon the role and importance of reason in guiding human actions and affairs. Argument is a very limited sense of the rational.

How might we return moral philosophy to its proper place of reasoning about the human condition? The ethics of categorical imperative and the utility of the greatest number come together in the program of "political correctness" that dominates our time. The doctrine of political correctness is a doctrine of intolerance that presents itself as a doctrine of perfect tolerance. Nothing noble, excellent, or self-determinate is allowed in the world of the politically correct. No action or form of speech is tolerated, in this world, that distinguishes majority from minority, one cultural tradition from another or the virtue of one individual over another. All eccentricity is excluded. There is no standard too low to endorse if it will keep all on the same plane, a principle expressed in the metaphor of all needing to be on a "level playing field."

When the doctrine of political correctness is coupled with the doctrine of "diversity," the intolerance of the divergent is complete. The doctrine of diversity presents itself as a high principle of democracy, in which all forms of the human condition are allowed. But, in fact, only those forms that fit a model of mass life are acceptable. The advocate of cultural diversity is a genius of mediocrity. All justice is social justice, that is, justice that is determined by acceptable political ideals, not justice as the absolute ideal of civil wisdom embodied in human law. In "social justice," "justice" does not function as a virtue because it is not used as a term to designate an excellence. "Justice" functions only as a placeholder for whatever relative values those employing the term intend it to mean. As a virtue, justice is a non-relative term, an absolute to which a human being or a society aspires. "Social justice" is a moral hoax.

Political correctness and diversity adjust the individual's comportment, thought, and speech to the mass that is inherent in the pursuit of the technological society. Once categorical imperative and utility are joined in a fixed doctrinal form, the need for purification is established, with the confidence that all that is eccentric or divergent can be conceived as forms of harassment, the modern term for heresy, and dealt with as unacceptable. The politically incorrect and non-diverse cannot be tolerated in public speech, in public actions, in the workplace, or in personal exchange and conversation. These are the enactments of modern society that confront the return of moral philosophy to its place as a field of human inquiry grounded in the human condition.

There are two ideas that reside at the center of ancient Greek and Latin moral philosophy and that were reasserted in the humanism of the Italian Renaissance: prudence and dignity. It is significant that modern ethics regards prudence as a second-rate or pseudo form of ethical action. Prudence is seen as a way to avoid ethical decision-making, a form of expediency or personal gain to resort to when all else fails. Dignity is a topic typically ignored in professional ethics, as it is tied to the idea of human nature, and for the modern thinker there is no such thing as human nature that lies beyond the relative conditions of human existence.

Neither prudence nor dignity is an agent of right, the basis of all deontological ethics and of ethical sense as found in modern society. For the Roman *Digest*, there is no such thing as a right that exists beyond the law. If there is a law that applies to a complaint, then there is a case; if not, there is no case. The law is in accord with human nature and is the teacher and repository of civil wisdom for society and the individual within it. Jurisprudence or the prudence of *ius*, or right, is the knowledge of the human condition itself. Thus the Romans claimed that what the Greeks called *philosophia*, they called *iurisprudentia*. The doctrine of natural rights, which achieved its modern formulation in the eighteenth century, descended in the development of the technological society, from its presence as life, liberty, and the pursuit of happiness, to take in the trivial forms characterized in "rights-talk."

Once the law is no more than an instrument of social justice, in other words, a form of politics as is claimed for all thought and social institutions in our time, a rights-claim can be attached to anything. Every dissatisfaction or complaint is a matter of one's rights. One has a right to everything. Once the claim of rights becomes free-floating as a means of testing laws, that is a kind of political jurisprudence, and then persons who feel disenfranchised can add the further claim of entitlement. Society is perceived as owing a debt to those within it who find themselves in some form of need. An entitlement is not earned or achieved by specific contribution to society; it is claimed of society, because society is thought to have failed certain persons or classes of persons and therefore must economically or "ethically" atone for its imperfections. Cicero says that what people have always sought is equality before the law. But the mentality of entitlement makes some, the "less fortunate," more equal than others, and, as Cicero says in *De officiis*, "For rights that are not open to all alike are no rights" (2.12).

The entitlement mentality regards those who have achieved self-sufficiency in society as simply more fortunate and considers that they should pay a little more than those less fortunate. Where one finds one's self in society is conceived as a matter of fortune, not intelligence, ability, or self-determination. The success of the claims to entitlement rests on the cultural endorsement of the ethics of the universality of the moral imperative and the utility of the greatest good for the greatest number. The states of existence that these abstract principles are held to engender are not in fact attainable. They thus depend upon the feeling of guilt that is generated by their constant failure to produce the perfect individual comportment and social governance. The guilt that accompanies the adoption of such abstract absolutes allows the phenomenon of entitlement to flourish and to invade and condition our lives. Giambattista Vico, the Italian philosopher of history, observed in one of the axioms of his new science of the common nature of the nations that "men first feel necessity, then look for utility, next attend to comfort, still later amuse themselves with pleasure, thence grow dissolute in luxury, and finally go mad and waste their substance" (axiom 66). We are in the process of reaching Vico's last stage.

Companion to the entitlement mentality is the mentality of the second chance. Within this mentality there is no possibility of failure or responsibility for it. It is the view that everyone deserves a second chance in regard to whatever one may have done—any act one commits that is morally wrong, any incompetence or discourtesy. Yet there is no such thing, on this view, as a true second chance, because any second chance functions as a new first chance, allowing for the indefinite expansion into any number of "second" chances. This indefinite expansion is another example of how Hegel's "bad infinity" is imbedded in social justice. There is no truly first chance. Because any first chance is always accompanied by a second chance, it has no stable meaning. The "second-chance" mentality is the mentality of excuses, transference of blame, and constant gerrymandering within the social system. The idea of charity and generosity toward the worthy poor and those truly in need is eliminated or so fully obscured that acts of human kindness appear eccentric and suspicious.

I wish to take the term "ethics" (*ēthika*) in its original sense, as found in Aristotle and earlier, as that which pertains to one's character, with character (*ethos*) understood as the product of habit. Heraclitus claims, "A man's *ēthos* is his *daimon*" (fr. 119). It is by habit directed by moral virtue that we acquire character, the basis for the practice of prudence, the end of which is *eudaimonia*, well-being, or, literally, the condition of having a good *daimon*. Because the modern term "ethics" has lost its connection with the philosophy of human nature and character, I prefer the term "moral philosophy." With the rise of the universities in Europe in the thirteenth century, the Aristotelian triad of ethics, economics, and politics became the structure for the moral philosophy curriculum. At the hands of the Renaissance humanists, moral philosophy found its place as one of the five fields of the *studia humanitatis*—the first two fields of the medieval *trivium*, grammar and rhetoric, added to the three supplementary fields of poetry, history, and moral philosophy. I am concerned with moral philosophy, not in its full triad but in only the first of the triad, ethics, keeping in mind that ethics is always part of what the ancients understood as politics, that is, the governance of the *polis*.

To the overlooked topic of dignity mentioned earlier, I wish to add that of the role of folly in human affairs. For an understanding of both of these I turn to the Renaissance. On folly and its connection to human wisdom, I rely on the insights of Sebastian Brant and Desiderius Erasmus, whose *Narrenschiff* and *Moriae Encomium* have been lost to moral philosophy. My concern with dignity is tied to two brief works: the "Oration on the Dignity of Man" of Giovanni Pico della Mirandola and the "Fable about Man" of Juan Luis Vives. No greater speeches on human dignity than these have been made.

In regard to prudence (*phronēsis*), I wish also to consider Cicero's conception of propriety (*decorum*) as crucial to human conduct. In so doing, let us approach ethics not as an extension of logic, but as first and foremost an extension of rhetoric as it effectively gives form to human affairs and human choice, understanding rhetoric as "the counterpart of dialectic," as Aristotle says in beginning the *Rhetoric*. Let us turn away from ethics as decision-making, whether based on imperative or utility, and return to the idea of moral choice as arising from the human itself and from the distinctly human pursuit of the well-being of the best life. It is worth our consideration, even if we conclude that we can comprehend it only imperfectly.

I am most grateful to my colleagues at Emory and other universities for their generosity in reading and commenting on this work in manuscript: Thora Bayer, Ann Hartle, George Benjamin Kleindorfer, Donald Livingston, David Lovekin, Frederick Marcus, and William Willeford. I thank Molly Black Verene for applying, in this work as in others, her indispensable talents to prepare it for press. Chapter 1, subsection on "Folly and the Modern World," and chapter 4 reprint texts that originally appeared in Donald Phillip Verene, *Philosophy and the Return to Self-Knowledge*, copyright 1997 by Yale University Press, used by permission.

Introduction: Moral Memory

EXPERIENCE AND COMMON SENSE tell us that we do not act morally because we have consulted a theory of ethics; we act morally in a given situation because of who we are. If part of who we are is the habit to comprehend intellectually what we do, then our actions involve reason. In acting morally the companion to reason is conscience. Conscience is that inner ability to sense right from wrong, just from unjust, the good from the bad. Conscience makes us what we are as moral agents; reason adds principles. Without conscience we are not capable of morally directed actions. The power of reason alone does not make us moral agents. Conscience and reason require the middle term of imagination. Without imagination conscience has no shape, and without imagination reason has no motivation. Imagination is an active force whereby the self sets an ideal for itself. The ideal must be felt from the power of empathy of conscience and must be thought from the power of reason to evaluate it. Thus we can speak of the moral imagination as the key to one's conduct as moral agent. But imagination does not stand on its own. It is part of the larger process of human memory, or, more specifically, that part of memory called recollection.

Recollection requires putting what is remembered into a sequence of causes in which things start from a beginning and one thing produces another. What has happened is re-collected as an intelligible sequence in which one thing leads in a meaningful way to another. Fundamental for us as moral agents is moral imagination, but more fundamental is moral memory. Nothing is imagined that is not in some sense already in memory. Our actions, including our moral actions, are always repetitions of what has gone before, although they differ in time and perhaps in place, and even in modality. Change in events is constant but it is never absolute. It is always a repetition and it always occurs through opposites. Moral action is action that occurs through moral opposites. Thus moral action is always guided by choice. Without choice there is no such action. But the choices we make have been made before. We need only remember them, and our memory of them is our guide when making a present or future choice.

Moral judgment, which is what guides moral choice, is not properly based on moral theory that is then applied to the specific situation. Moral judgment is memorial. It is generated and grounded in the apprehension of principles present in past moral action. Moral judgment is the application of the past to the present, with anticipation of its effects on the future. All moral judgment is dialectical in the sense that it reflects an order of change through opposites in time. Moral judgment is a way to think time in logical terms such that choice can be made. Choice, once made, enters back into memory to become the basis of future judgment.

How are we to put aside the idea of applied ethics, which understands moral choice and moral action as the application of theoretical principles to a specific problem, argued out in pro-and-con fashion, with a true picture of human morality? Applied ethics is an activity of academics, not of citizens acting within their own civic lives. How can we restore thought about morals to the vivacity of the human condition and connect ethics to the actual world? The applied ethicists pride themselves on the fact that in their claims they are addressing real-world problems, but they never are. Their analyses always have a rarified air about them. Their thoughts are always technical. They never speak from what it means to be human. To grasp the human requires the language of a literate perspective, thought informed by the world of letters, as it has developed in and resides in human culture.

The remarks that follow purport to arise from just such a humane perspective, connected to ordinary experience. The reader should be warned that these are no more than introductory remarks, intended only to point out what is in the theater of the world in which we live. They may test the reader's patience, and the reader may wish to pass on to some other philosophical way of speaking that is more familiar, and avoid such meditations. Should such be the case, I bear the reader no malice. Not all forms of thinking are for everyone.

We may say that morality, as well as good sense, is the best distributed thing in the world, for all think themselves so well endowed with both that even those who are hardest to please in everything else do not usually desire more of them than they possess. We may also say that not only the synthesis of thought and sensation but morality, too, is an art, concealed in the depths of the human soul, whose real modes of activity nature is hardly likely ever to allow us to discover and to have open to our gaze. This is because morality, as well as metaphysics, is the finding of bad reasons for what we believe upon instinct, but to find these reasons is no less an instinct.

Every moral act is a fable for us, in brief. It is not a fable in the sense of something untrue, but a fable in its original sense of a true narration. Such a fable requires that we can recall it at will to inform us in future moral acts. The power of ingenuity is added to this recall in order to perceive the verisimilitude in things, such that one act can be placed in its proper arrangement with another that is held in memory—and memory, as Aristotle tells us, is the same as imagination (*phantasia*).[1] Memory, then, is the heart of morality. Our moral acts are held together by memory in the sense of recollection, in which one act is recalled so as to account for another. And so our moral persona or character is produced. The moral must be grasped in terms of its own inner form. Once realized in its own form, the moral must be comprehended as a form of self-knowledge within the whole of human culture.

Morality exists for the reason religion exists—because of the human condition. The human condition is mortality. Mortality is not a property of the pantheon of gods of any society, because the gods are not mortal. Their very existence is not a problem for them. Even if the divine is the source of all goodness, the existence of the divine Godhead is not a question for it. The gods are the archetypes of the human imagination and as such they are immortal forms. They exist outside temporality. Human beings exist in time and they share mortality with animals but animals do not share the human condition. Animals are mortal but their mortality is not a condition of their awareness of what it is to exist. Animals live lives but they do not know that they do. Thus animals do not seek self-knowledge. Human beings stand between the models of immortality of the gods or the Godhead and the thoughtless existence of the world of animals.

Once human beings find themselves in time, they face the question of their own existence. Two passions govern their response: fear and shame. They fear the ever-presence of their own individual end, their mortality, and they judge their own actions. What one does determines what one is, and what one is determines how one confronts one's mortality. Decorum or propriety—that is, how one proportions one's acts—allows for and establishes the courage to confront mortality. If morality requires narration, shame is what we wish to avoid in the moral relation of our acts, whether to ourselves or to others. Character allows us to conquer fear and to avoid shame. What character is to the individual, tradition is to the community or the nation. Character and tradition define decorum. Without decorum there is no inner form to the self. Self-knowledge requires that the self be always more than it is at any moment or given set of conditions.

---

1. Aristotle, *On Memory* 450a.

Thus the human condition, unlike the purely animal condition, is always more than the present. What is in the present depends on what is in memory, and what is in memory determines what is to come. The moral act is generated by the formation and presence of the ideal. Without the ideal there is nothing but the present for the self. In the ideal the self is constantly going beyond itself in an effort to overcome fear and to avoid the shameful. The ideal is unknown to animal life and it is not a necessary condition for the immortal life of the gods or the Godhead. The ideal generates choice, which is the basis of morality. The gods do whatever they wish and the Godhead is itself simply moral; its actions are not the result of moral deliberation and choice.

Francesco Guicciardini, the Florentine historian, says in his *Ricordi*: "All that which has been in the past and is at present will be again in the future. But both the names and the appearances of things change, so that he who does not have a good eye will not recognize them. Nor will he know how to grasp a norm of conduct or make a judgment by means of observation."[2] Guicciardini's "good eye," his *buono occhio*, is the key to moral judgment, and moral judgment is the key to the moral act. But further, both of these require moral memory. To learn the art of memory we must associate ourselves with the Muses, who are the daughters of Mnemosyne. The Muses are said by Hesiod to know how to sing many false songs but also to sing true songs when they will. Their eloquence, like human speech itself, points in both directions. The power of their speech allows them to tell of things past, things present, and things to come, in a harmonious voice. They instructed Hesiod always to place the Muses at the beginning and at the end of his song. In this way the poet's song may confront the work of Cronus, the maker of time. Myth and music are instruments for the obliteration of time.[3] In them, time does not escape the harmony of the circle in which time returns upon itself. The Heliconian Muses are said to dance around the altar of the son of Cronus, that is, Zeus, who is their father.

Augustine connects time to song by using the example of a *psalmos*, the Greek rendering of the Hebrew *mizmōr*. He says: "We do not measure poems by pages, for that would be to measure space not time; we measure by the way the voice moves in uttering the poem." The mind has three kinds of acts, Augustine says: "the mind expects, attends, and remembers: what it expects passes, by way of what it attends to, into what it remembers." Further, he says: "Suppose that I am about to recite a psalm that I know. Before I begin, my expectation is directed to the whole of it; but when I have begun,

2. Guicciardini, *Ricordi*, 131. My translation.
3. Lévi-Strauss, *Raw and the Cooked*, 16.

so much of it as I pluck off and drop away into the past becomes matter for my memory; and the whole energy of the action is divided between my memory, in regard to what I have said, and my expectation, in regard to what I will say."

Augustine continues: "But there is a present act of attention, by which what was future passes on its way to becoming past. The further I go in my recitation, the more my expectation is diminished and my memory lengthened, until the whole of my expectation is used up when the action is completed and has passed wholly into my memory." He concludes: "And what is true of the whole psalm, is true for each part of the whole, and for each syllable: and likewise for any larger action, of which the canticle may be only a part: indeed it is the same for the whole life of man, of which all a man's actions are parts: and likewise for the whole history of the human race, of which all the lives of men are parts."[4]

What the Muses teach in the Greco-Roman world is taught in the psalm of the Judeo-Christian tradition. When the mind holds something in its attention, it makes it possible for what is to come to pass into what was. A song is never sung only once; songs achieve their truth by repetition. Repetition trains the mind in attention. It is this attention to repetition that allows us to grasp a norm of conduct. Just as any event is part of a pattern that exists in time, so any particular moral situation has existed in essence before, exists now, and will exist again. The art of the moral act, as mentioned above, is that of verisimilitude, of seeing the connection between things that otherwise may seem unconnected. It requires the kind of genius or wit that is expressed in the power of *ingenium*.

Ingenium is not convertible into *method*. It can be learned only by imitation of nature. If we would master the moral act, we must first master metaphor. For, as Aristotle says, "the greatest thing by far is to be a master of metaphor. It is the one thing that cannot be learnt from others; and it is also a sign of genius, since a good metaphor implies an intuitive perception of the similarity in dissimilars."[5] As in poetry and morals, so it is in the law—we must apprehend the similarities in dissimilars. To act morally we must base our actions on a precedent case that informs that which confronts us. As the poet Giuseppe Ungaretti tells us, with complete clarity, "*Tutto, tutto, tutto è memoria*" ("Everything, everything, everything is memory").[6] Without memory we cannot hold what is before us as a repeatable image so

---

4. Augustine, *Confessions*, 227–30.

5. Aristotle, *Poetics* 1459a.

6. Ungaretti, *Vite*, 345.

that we can recall what is at issue and hold it before us for our comprehension in rational terms.

To think about a problematic situation by placing it before the mind in terms of rational principles, that is, to apprehend it purely conceptually, even connecting the concept to evidence that supports its meaning, is to miss the music essential to any human event. The proportions of the event, or its music, must be grasped, and this grasping requires its connections to its past and its likely future. The event is not open-ended; it is always a circle such that in its beginning is its end. What is true in an event can be grasped only by grasping the event as a whole. As Francis Bacon writes in his essay "Of Vicissitude of Things": "Solomon saith, 'There is no new thing upon the earth.' So that as Plato had an imagination, that 'all knowledge was but remembrance,' so Solomon giveth his sentence, that 'all novelty is but oblivion.' Whereby you may see the river of Lethe runneth as well above ground as below."[7] No situation is truly novel, for if it were, by definition, it could not be known. Only what is remembered can be known, and it can be known only in terms of what has been known, that is, what is remembered. What is to come is only that which is capable of entering memory, or it would have no relation to its own origin.

In the matter of memory, we should not neglect to note that education is memory. What is acquired by the mind when educated is held in memory. To be educated is to have the ability to call forth the ideas, evidences, sources, and authorities drawn from culture stored in the treasure-house of topics in the mind and apply them to an issue at hand. Moral education is no exception. Moral choice is educated choice involving the same ability as educated thinking generally. Educated thought generally may aim only at comprehension of an issue without the additional aim of acting on such knowledge. Morally motivated thought has the aim of comprehension but has the further aim of choice and action in relation to an issue.

Education is not simply critical thinking, because *ars critica* necessarily presupposes *ars topica*. We must first draw forth, from what is in memory, what is needed to comprehend an issue. Only then can we intelligently apply the powers of criticism to the issue and proceed toward choice and action. The rhetorical art of topics is always presupposed by the logical art of critical principles. Critical thinking, whether its practitioner knows it or not, always employs topics, as the points from which to think and analyze what experience gives. Morality requires education in the sense of *paideia* or *Bildung*, that is, education not in the sense of training or acquisition of information

---

7. Bacon, "Vicissitude," 451. Borges, "Immortal," 183, uses these lines as an epigraph.

but in the sense of the development of the human spirit within the self, the inculcation of human culture into the individual's existence as a self.

If we think apart from memory, there is nothing to guide us in the moral act, as Hegel has explained in the *Philosophy of Right*: "For the proposition 'Consider whether your maxim can be asserted as a universal principle' would be all very well if we already had determinate principles concerning how to act. In other words, if we demand of a principle that it should be able to serve as the determinant of a universal legislation, this presupposes that it already has a content; and if this content were present, it would be easy to apply the principle. But in this case, the principle itself is not yet available, and the criterion that there should be no contradiction is non-productive—for where there is nothing, there can be no contradiction either."[8]

Logical consistency cannot provide a guide for moral action, as Hegel makes clear at the beginning of the *Science of Logic*. Something is the same as nothing, since something is the idea of complete indeterminacy, and complete indeterminacy is the precise definition of nothing.[9] When a principle can be applied universally to everything, its opposite can be equally well applied. The moral act in fact presupposes the existence of an ethical community within which the act can occur, be related, and be judged. The commonalities upon which human community rests depend upon memory. As Hegel says in the *Philosophy of Right*: "In an ethical community, it is easy to say *what* someone must do and *what* the duties are which he has to fulfill in order to be virtuous."[10] What is said of a universal maxim asserted directly from reason holds also for a maxim based on the utility of the greatest good for the greatest number. Both require the presence of an ethical community with its tradition, and tradition is always actualized human memory.

Utility presupposes a community, but not simply a community in general, or a universal community. Utility requires standards of conduct that are established by and in the community as necessary to its good and well-being. Thus the act that is judged moral is determined in accord with what is actually present and endorsed by the community. These standards are preserved in the customs and the laws of the community. Commonalities are always poetic. They attempt to hold the dissimilar together through the similar, and in so doing they attempt to deny time—to offer a permanence against meaningless change. What Mircea Eliade, in *The Myth of the Eternal Return*, calls the "terror of history" is for the individual to face a

---

8. Hegel, *Philosophy of Right*, 163.

9. Hegel, *Science of Logic*, chap. 1.

10. Hegel, *Philosophy of Right*, 193.

deontological world in which all judgments are made in terms of ongoing situations, the principles of which derive directly from applied universals.

The community and the moral act within it require an ontological ground. True community is always an instantiation of the *summum bonum*, of the Good that is beyond time and to which time is subject by the persistence of the community. The Good does not function as a ground for freedom from time. It is a ground for freedom in the sense of self-determination. What is in time is not self-determined and is thus not free—that is, if time is grasped as historical time, as one event passing into another, rather than the past, present, and future forming a circle, as we find in Augustine's treatment of time. Our grasp of the eternal return of the circle of time requires a grasp of the Good as beyond time, an absolute standard to which time must answer. The freedom of the individual is based on imitation of the self-determination of the Good as an ultimate standard of freedom. Freedom is not freedom from temporal succession but freedom to act within this succession by connecting to what is without it.

Moral action requires the sense of the ideal, not in the sense of an abstract end but in the sense of a human type that is formed by the imagination from the study of history and literature. It is to the poets that we must look for such figures, but not in the sense that the poets themselves can tell us what is moral in the figures that inhabit their works. The same can be said of the historians, the poets being the first historians in their activity of retelling the primordial myths. We must approach poetry and history with moral intention already in place. They will not produce it for us, for poetry and history produce whatever can be found in the human condition, regardless of its moral goodness or lack of it.

A. W. Levi, in his discussion of the moral imagination, makes this clear: "Only our human species can examine nature and history, desire better things, and form an ideal. Every significant epoch in the history of the West, therefore has a moral program and an aim, an ambition which its choicest spirits have set before them and striven to reach. The realm of choices and endeavors is always guided by an ideal, and the expression of this ideal is symbolized by a paradigm—a way of life which constitutes that epoch's standard of moral excellence and spiritual attainment." Levi says further: "The complete story of moral idealism as it informs the course of Western culture from the Greeks to our own age is the record of successive ideal conceptions of the living of the good life, of ideals of personality and character, changing from period to period, yet recurring memorably in ages which have otherwise outgrown them."[11] What can be discerned in

11. Levi, *High Road of Humanity*, 17.

Western culture can be discerned in other cultures, in the sense that human culture itself depends upon the ideal and so does moral action with it, no matter how widely such ideals may vary. The moral act presupposes cultural memory, for it is only by such memory and the education of the individual in it that a reflective stance can be attained on one's own age. As William Faulkner claims, in his well-known assertion: "The past is never dead. It's not even past."[12] Ideals that we require to act as human beings lie in our imagination, that is, memory, for, as noted earlier, "imagination is memory." Ideals are the mirrors held up by the mind before its eye, in which we can see ourselves in terms of the moral possibilities we seek. Even when the ideal is not consciously present to us, when we engage in the moral act, it is there. If all books are always about other books and all works of art rest on earlier art, whether known to the artist or not, all moral action rests on other moral action that can be reached by memory as an ideal.

The moral act is guided not solely by the memorial ideal but also by the power of reason to grasp the whole of a situation and to make distinctions within it. There is a dialectic between the image held in memory and formed by the imagination and the reflective and speculative powers of reason to analyze it and apply it to what is present as a moral issue for the individual. The telos is set by the image but the way to it is set by reasoning. The individual is always faced by the themes of Robert Frost's poem "The Road Not Taken"—of two roads, taking the one less traveled makes all the difference. The moral act is always the search for the road less traveled by, once the morality of a situation transcends custom. If it does not, and adheres to custom, then the choice is the road most traveled and the moral issue was just temporary. If custom provides no road the moral act must seek the road less traveled, which will make all the difference. And this road depends on the interaction of memory and reason.

Memory must be understood, not as simple recall or Proustian memory, where a sensation in the present sets off a series of scenes from the past, although such recovery of lost time is a natural and necessary beginning point for the introduction of memory into the present. As noted earlier, memory as the basis for the moral act requires memory in the sense of recollection. This means that the things remembered and formed by the imagination must be put into a proper order. Aristotle defines recollection in this sense: "when one wishes to recollect, that is what he will do: he will try to obtain a beginning of movement whose sequel shall be the movement which he desires to reawaken. This explains why attempts at recollection

12. Faulkner, *Requiem for a Nun*, act 1, scene 3.

succeed soonest and best when they start from a beginning."[13] To recollect requires the location of the beginning of a thing and the formation of it in the mind as it develops from its past to the present and anticipates a future.

It is no accident that the moral act and memory in the sense of recollection are both powers distinctive to the human being. To remember and to respond morally are to live in time. Aristotle says: "the object of memory is the past. All memory, therefore, implies a time elapsed; consequently only those animals which perceive time remember, and the organ whereby they perceive time is also that whereby they remember."[14] The human animal is both in time and has power over time. In the *History of Animals*, Aristotle says: "Many animals have memory, and are capable of instruction; but no other creature except man can recall the past at will."[15]

Vico, thinking from Aristotle, says that memory has three aspects: "memory [*memoria*] when it remembers things, imagination [*fantasia*] when it alters or imitates them, and ingenuity [*ingegno*] when it gives them a new turn or puts them into proper arrangement and relationship."[16] Ingenuity (*ingegno*; Latin *ingenium*) is the third capability that is necessary for the moral act. The imagination arrests time in the image, but to act in terms of what the imagination forms requires the connection of what is formed with all else that is relevant. Ingenuity is the antithesis of method. Ingenuity finds order by the perception of commonalities in what is otherwise dissimilar. Once a commonality is found, it brings with it the possibility that a method can be formulated whereby the commonality can be reproduced and elaborated over and over. Ingenuity requires a natural talent of perception that can be enhanced by example and by imitation, but it cannot be taught or attained in any didactic sense. Method can be taught. It can be learned by systematic instruction in relation to a given subject matter. But ingenuity gives us the subject matter itself. Thus ingenuity (*ingenium*) is tied to invention (*inventio*), and in this tie it is necessary to the finding of beginning points for thought and for action based upon thought.

Political correctness, diversity, entitlement, and second chance-ism lie outside moral memory because they are not truly moral ideas. They are purely political ideas that are allowed to fill out the empty space in moral thought left by the abstractions of deontological and utilitarian ethics. The term "political correctness" is apt because, as a principle of moral activity, it turns all that would be proper to morality into politics. Politics rightly

---

13. Aristotle, *On Memory* 451b.

14. Ibid. 449b.

15. Aristotle, *History of Animals* 488b.

16. Vico, *New Science*, 313–14.

pertains to the activity of the state. Political thoughts and actions are governed principally by expediency. Morals pertain to the actions of individuals and relations among individuals. When such actions are understood only in terms of political doctrines, the individual disappears into the mass. The liberality necessary to individual self-determination and responsibility is replaced by a covert and subtle sense of political dominance. Once politics becomes the ultimate frame of reference for human activity, dominance of the individual is complete. Morality is no longer a manifestation of a transcendent standard to which human conduct can aspire. Justice, that most transcendent of virtues, becomes social justice. And wisdom—that virtue attached to the pursuit of truth—becomes social wisdom, or ideology.

Once the political has replaced the moral, there is no opportunity for the moral to rise from the individual to influence the expedient decisions and actions of the state. The ideologies of political correctness, diversity, entitlement, and second chance-ism are duplicitous at their core. The abstract perfect conditions of human interchange they depict can never be realized. They must constantly be redefined. This redefinition is driven by suspicion. There is the ever-present suspicion that the language and policies they engender are not fully correct. Thus the physical infirmities and mental deficiencies that naturally befall various individuals must be spoken of in terms that are constantly revised, with the aim of making such defects appear superlative to the norm. The same process is applied to any differences between races, cultures, and social and economic classes. All is constantly redefined, such that differences that are actual and carrying their own inherent value are reduced to the same plane of meaning and merged into a single sense of social life. The duplicity lies in the fact that any intelligent individual knows that these differences are real and that they determine much of what occurs in the human world, out of sight of the pseudo-moral mentality of political correctness, diversity, and so forth.

In any society in which the individual has opportunities to pursue economic success and human happiness, everyone deserves, and has, a first chance to engage in such pursuits. But if the individual squanders such opportunities, it is left to the individual to confront failure, on the basis of character. The mentality of second chance-ism regards failure, not as the responsibility of the individual, but of the society. Nothing is expected of the individual—neither strength of character nor admission of failure. Everyone deserves a second chance, on this view, regardless of the person's worthiness or effort. The claim of second chance thus becomes a claim of a right the individual has, based only on the claim that the society has somehow failed the individual, not that the individual has failed. The consciousness of the second chance is an ever-extended pattern of self-deception and social duplicity.

If the reader has had the patience and generosity to bear with these remarks to this point, it will be evident that they do not constitute an argument, with premises leading to a conclusion. They are preliminary remarks that are generated from a view that I wish to convey more systematically in Part 1. A. N. Whitehead held that "it is more important that a proposition be interesting than that it be true. The importance of truth is, that it adds to interest."[17] My aim in what follows is to portray moral thinking in relation to the human condition rather than to resolve particular moral problems. In so doing I wish to refract moral sensibilities in various ways and place them against the realities of modern existence.

17. Whitehead, *Process and Reality*, 395–96.

PART 1

The Practice of Prudence

INTRODUCTORY REMARKS

WHEN IONESCO'S *RHINOCEROS* WAS performed in 1960, first in Paris and then in London, the bankruptcy of modern ethics reached the imagination of the literate public of the Gallic and Anglo-Saxon worlds. In the play, the figures, who represent various persons in ordinary life, progressively transform themselves into rhinos, in order to go with the times. The ethics of Kantian duty and the Utilitarian ethics of happiness for the greatest number prove to be no match for the sudden arrival and then continuing presence of rhino existence.

The rhino relieves the residents of the village in which the play is set of the inconvenience and responsibilities of being human. The human condition is transcended and a new principle of herd existence is realized in its place. A new social order is brought into being. The speeches of the village Logician inquiring into the types and definition of rhinos show the comedy of claiming that argument can allow us to comprehend the new order or to direct our choice to become or not to become a rhino.

So great is the attraction of the rhino order of things that, at the end of the play, only one human being, Berenger, is holding out. He declares he is the last man left and that he is staying that way and not capitulating. The audience is left with this uncertain image of the "last man," but with no indication of the ground upon which he can continue to stand and not capitulate.

It is unclear from Ionesco's play what the rhinos are intended to be, as transformed human entities. They at least symbolize the banality of power. They make individuality unnecessary. Once one is a rhino, it is unnecessary to be anything more. Those in the audience who are not, in some sense, already rhinos are in Berenger's position. Ionesco may have had totalitarian politics in mind, with his symbolism of the rhinos, but we might just as well associate it with the herd instinct and politics of the politically correct and the politics of diversity that would force all into their mold—their intolerance toward any views outside their own.

Is there any ground upon which we may stand, once we have given up the *summum bonum,* and face the human condition in terms of our own devising—that is, in terms of rational imperative, utility, and choice directed by pro-and-con argument? To answer this question, we may proceed in the way we may proceed in regard to any philosophical question—to look at what we have forgotten that is already there, in the history of our mental culture.

1

The Moral in the Theater of the World

THE MORAL ACT AND ITS NARRATION

A T FIRST, MORALITY IS habit. Children delight in imitation. They form their actions on the basis of what is present to them in others. Their actions are disciplined by parents, relatives, and friends, that is, if they are fortunate to have those who themselves are guided by virtue and decorum. Habits, when they come together in the individual as a coherent whole, form character. Thus character arises naturally from the self's relation to itself and as the basis for the relation of the self to others. The habits of the individual confront social habits or customs, and the child finds itself in a world of manners and moral order.

If the world of family and friends is not present for the child as a world of civilized life and moral expectation, the child has no or little basis for shaping natural desires and appetites or developing judgment and willpower to direct actions. That child experiences no sense of excellence and is potentially an unfortunate or dangerous human being. But the lack of proper conditions to develop as a human being of character does not mean the child has no chance to acquire character and thus is excused from moral or legal restraint. Experience shows that many who are deprived of a proper childhood find a way to rectify this early deprivation and arrive in adulthood as individuals of good character. Others do not and are lost to their own potential humanity. Why one individual surmounts difficult conditions of origin and another does not but is submerged in them is a question that remains without a clear answer. This view of childhood is not intended as a social-scientific account of child development but only as a general picture of the human.

When a child reaches the age of reason morality transcends habit and reflective morality begins to take shape. By this time conscience also becomes active, the child having been repeatedly exhorted to exercise empathy in relation to others by the question, How would you feel if someone acted in such and such a manner to you as you are acting toward them?

When habits and customs conflict within themselves, offering the individual no clear course of action in a given situation, reflection enters as a means to establish choice. Reflection is the method of the understanding. The understanding approaches the world by means of classifying its contents and formulating critical judgments concerning truth and error in regard to what is held about these contents. Reflective morality is tied to the phenomenon of arguments pro and con in relation to a given issue or problematic situation, in an effort to direct choice. But within this approach to the moral, duplicity reigns. The self, now capable of constructing arguments and placing them over habits and customs, holds fast to the claim that such arguments can in principle and thus in fact direct choice, when actually moral choice is generated through the force of character and a specific moral argument is endorsed on the basis of what the individual will do because of who the individual in fact is.

To overcome the inherent self-duplicity of reflective morality, what I will call speculative morality is required. Speculative morality does not rely on the antimony of argument and counterargument, nor is it a reversion to habit and custom. Speculative morality rests on the acknowledgment that character and choice are dialectically related. The moral agent must see with the mind's eye the connection between character and choice in any moral action. What is required is not the critical and analytic powers of the understanding but the synthetic power of reason, the power to perceive the connection between character and choice in a given instance as reasonable. Morality, then, is what we tell ourselves after we have acted. Faced with a moral situation that requires us to act, we act from the basis of our character. We must choose, knowingly choose, and choose from the consistency of our character. Choice requires that we not act under such extreme duress that only one course of action is truly open to us. The key to our choice is narration.

We must act, and in acting we must be able to relate to ourselves why we have so acted. We must rely on reason to keep us from simply providing ourselves with a rationalization. Rationalization is subjective reasoning that appears objective. But reason aims at objectivity. To be objective is to attempt to ground the elements of our decision, choice, or action in the whole of things. This narration guided by reason that is formed to justify our action presupposes a narration of the problematic situation itself. To act when confronted by a problematic situation we must first assess what will be the natural course of the events involved: what is its origin, its present state, and its future end, to the extent these can be grasped. The situation must be apprehended as a whole. Only then can we act, and once we have acted we must be able to place our action within a new relation of the whole. In this way, by rational narration, we build up a moral self, for all situations have been before in some form, are now, and will be again.

Reason and narration are counterparts because both are ways of giving form to the whole. The understanding functions as a means to dissect, classify, and connect what is partial in experience. The counterpart to the understanding is the proposition. Propositions connect this to that. Thus reflective morality is always seeking a decision procedure in order to determine what should be done, what should be connected to what to make the right choice. But the key to narration is the story. All stories, if they are fully told, produce a whole before our imagination. Stories, like songs, are wholes that hold all their elements in proportion to each other. A rational narration is not simply a history; it holds all of its elements together as an order *per causas*. In this manner what is related is comprehended as having a total order in which all elements are dialectically interrelated. A rational narration informs us not only of what has occurred but also why it has occurred.

Reflection and speculation are two ways of seeing. Reflection separates the mind's eye from its object and determines its form as separate from its act of knowing. Reflection, as its Latin root, *reflectere*, tells us, is to turn our gaze back from the object, to apprehend it by retreating from it to a position outside its reality. Speculation, as its Latin root *specere* suggests, is to see into or spy out the inner form of its object. We apprehend the object by entering into its inner reality. We apprehend it by attempting to become it. Our penetration of its inner form is a kind of imitation of it as opposed to a reflective pointing out of it. Our moral act is predicated on our form of knowing. Once we know rightly, we can choose rightly. This sense of choice requires that we pass through reflective morality to speculative morality, and speculative morality requires that we join our powers of imagination with those of reason.

The motivation to engage in the moral narration of our acts after we have acted is rooted in the phenomenon of conscience. Conscience is considered in chapter 3, but its role is also of importance here. What conscience is, is lost in the depths of the human psyche, but that conscience exists in those individuals who have acquired a moral sense in their development as human selves is beyond dispute. Conscience is often associated with guilt. One may have a guilty conscience concerning a past action and be moved to relieve this burden of guilt from one's life by some manner of restitution or atonement. Conscience, however, is a wider agency than the feeling of personal guilt. Conscience is based in empathy. Empathy is the distinctively human capacity for participating in another's feelings, volitions, or life situation. It depends upon the ability imaginatively to project a subjective state onto another and to respond to it. It is the key to speculative morality because to exercise empathy one must see into the inner state of another and be affected by this vision.

This insight into the other is based on the self-insight that is at the base of conscience. This self-insight is a sense of right or wrong within the individual. Conscience is an inner power that guides the individual's action toward goodness and toward justice, both in relation to the other and for the other, within the other's situation. Conscience is tied to consciousness; these two terms in English share the common Latin root of *conscientia*. Our consciousness of our selves is connected to our consciousness of others and our necessary involvement with them as not only knowing animals but also as social animals. Conscience originates from consciousness when consciousness becomes a witness to the other. When this witnessing consciousness proceeds from observing the other to engaging in its capacity for empathy for the other, the result is conscience as an active force within the self.

In the *Second Discourse*, Rousseau writes, "It is very certain, therefore, that pity is a natural sentiment which, moderating in each individual the activity of love of oneself, contributes to the mutual preservation of the entire species."[1] *La pitié* is pity, in the sense of compassion. Compassion is the result of empathy governed by conscience. It is a natural sentiment that stands over and against the Hobbesian view of "a generall inclination of all mankind, a perpetuall and restlesse desire of Power after power, that ceaseth only in Death."[2]

I hold that both the sentiment of pity or compassion and the perpetual desire of power are natural to the human condition. Within the human individual these two opposites stand in dialectical relation. Between them conscience is a middle term. We are capable of being drawn to the other by pity or compassion based on our power of empathy. But we are also drawn to the other by our desire for dominance. This desire is held in check by conscience because when we apprehend ourselves as moral agents the

1. Rousseau, *First and Second Discourses*, 132–33.
2. Hobbes, *Leviathan*, 161.

narration we form for our actions is a story of compassion that modifies our inclination to self-aggrandizement. Compassion for the other is not the only course of moral action. If we are threatened by the other—for example, by the terrorist, as discussed in chapter 2—prudence requires us to draw upon the capacity of power that is otherwise held in check during conditions of peaceful existence. To unleash our exertion of power toward the other requires that such desire is perpetually present. But as moral agents we must, after we have acted, form a rational narration that justifies our prudent action such that it was not simply expedient but was right—that our action of self-defense or preservation was in accord with virtue and our own humanity.

Conscience is what keeps the moral narrative rational rather than a rationalization. Conscience is not only the basis in the individual for directing the individual's actions rightly in relation to others, and for keeping the mind's eye on the good, it is the basis for self-honesty. The risk inherent in any particular moral narrative that is formed to comprehend and justify one's actions is that it may be self-deceptive. Any such narrative may be incomplete or defective in some aspects, but if it is self-deceptive it is useless. The individual can only appeal to the natural sentiments of conscience to attempt to avoid the self-deception inherent in rationalization.

The appeal to conscience is a habit that is central to the development of character. To ignore or put aside the presence of conscience is to substitute expediency for prudence, for expediency does not take right and wrong as ultimates that govern human action. It takes right and wrong as relative to a given set of conditions. Expedient action may attempt to choose the best course, but the sense of the best, in this case, is simply pragmatic. Prudent action judges the pragmatic by the standard of excellence expressed in the pantheon of virtues that are embodiments of the good. The path of virtue in any given case may not be pragmatic in any immediate sense; thus such a path may be inexpedient. Ultimately, however, the path of virtue is pragmatic, in the sense that it leads to the good life, and its requirement that the individual make no one the worse for knowing him. A life governed by expediency may be to some extent in accord with the dictates of conscience, but ultimately it is not good unless it is accidentally good. If the good life is good in essence it is governed by moral excellence, the standard for which depends upon the individual's grasp of the meaning of the virtues as embodiments of the good.

Aristotle has put the point of the prominence of the moral act in the most perfect terms: "It is well said, then, that as a result of doing just things, the just person comes into being and as a result of doing moderate things, the moderate person; without performing these actions, nobody would become good." He further explains why argument is not a substitute for moral action nor for moral philosophy: "Yet most people [the *hoi polloi*] do not do them; and, seeking refuge in argument, they suppose they are philosophizing and that they will in this way be serious." He says such people are like those who when ill listen attentively to their physicians but do nothing prescribed. Such persons "will not have a body in good condition by caring for it in this way, so too the former will not have a soul in good condition by philosophizing in this way."[3] We become moral by performing moral actions.

SAPIENTIA, ELOQUENTIA, PRUDENTIA

In Renaissance Italian humanism, an ideal that was held in highest regard was "*la sapienza che parla*" or "wisdom speaking." Wisdom or sapience is to think any subject as a whole, and eloquence is to put this whole into words. Once this connection between thought and language can be done in regard to a subject or problem, effective and proper action can be taken, should any action be required. Thus wisdom speaking is the key to prudent action. The practice of prudence is not self-contained; it is generated by and depends upon the interconnection between thought and speech. *Sapientia*, *eloquentia*, and *prudentia* are parallel to the claim Horace makes for *ars poetica*—that it should instruct, delight, and move.[4] Cicero also claims these three functions for *ars oratoria*.[5] In speaking in a public forum or in court, the speaker must be able to affect the audience in these three ways. Otherwise the speech, like the poem, is incomplete and ineffective.

If we ask what each of these terms means in this triad, we may turn to Cicero, Quintilian, and Vico. In the *Tusculan Disputations* Cicero says: "Wisdom [*sapientia*] is the knowledge of things divine and human and acquaintance with the cause of each of them."[6] He repeats this claim in *De officiis*, saying that *sapientia* has been defined this way "by the philosophers of old."[7] Indeed, in the *Apology* Socrates says that he is perhaps wise in human wisdom and that others he has questioned may have a greater wisdom than the human, but if so he does not understand it.[8] In the *Charmides* and the *Phaedrus* Socrates says he is not a maker of theories but a seeker of the

3. Aristotle, *Ethics* 1105b.

4. Horace, *Ars poetica* 333.

5. Cicero, *Brutus* 185.

6. Cicero, *Tusculan Disputations* 4.26.57.

7. Cicero, *De officiis* 2.2.5.

8. Plato, *Apology* 20d–e.

wisdom that resides in the self and that concerns the knowledge of things human and divine.[9] From this Socratic approach we can form the principle that wisdom or sapience has as its object what is human, but beyond the human is the divine, with which we have at best indirect acquaintance. Thus wisdom as human knowledge includes ignorance of what is beyond the human. The whole is not self-sufficient as an object of thought, for we never perfectly grasp its limits or the nature of these limits. In this sense our wisdom of the whole involves wonder or *thauma*, and, as Aristotle says, this *thauma* originates from the experience of *aporia* in thought. Our thought is never self-contained. Thus our thought never attains certainty in thinking the whole.[10]

In speaking the whole our speech is complete but imperfect. In *Institutio oratoria* Quintilian says: "The verb *eloqui* means the production and communication to the audience of all that the speaker has conceived in his mind, and without this power all the preliminary accomplishments of oratory are as useless as a sword that is kept permanently concealed within its sheath."[11] Eloquence is not simply the formation of elegant and ornate phrases. Eloquence does require *copia*, in that it joins together many aspects of its subject. Eloquence is synthetic speech that has within it vision that goes to the limits of the whole. As Longinus, in *On the Sublime*, says, "a well-timed flash of sublimity shatters everything like a bolt of lightning and reveals the full power of the speaker at a single stroke."[12] Cicero was renowned for the felicity of his copiousness, and Demosthenes could speak of quite distant things, going outside his case only to bring his audience back with the lightning flash of his mighty enthymeme.

In *On the Study Methods of Our Time*, Vico says: "There is only one 'art of prudence' and this art is philosophy."[13] Vico is alluding to the first line of the *Digest* of Roman law, which claims that jurisprudence is true philosophy.[14] The prudence of the law or jurisprudence is the guide to human conduct. The laws are our teachers because they reflect the essence of human order and reason in human affairs. Laws are not conceived as deterrents to actions we would naturally do but as guides we would naturally seek in order to act in a virtuous manner. As Vico claims, Roman law was originally a "severe poem," and citing Cicero, he reminds us that the most

9. Plato, *Charmides* 169e; *Phaedrus* 230a.

10. Aristotle, *Metaphysics* 982b.

11. Quintilian, *Institutio oratoria* 8. pr. 15–16.

12. Longinus, *On the Sublime* 1.4.

13. Vico, *Study Methods*, 77.

14. Justinian, *Digest* 1.1.

ancient version of Roman law, the Law of the Twelve Tables, was originally a song that was sung by children on the streets of Rome.[15] In *De partitione oratoria*, Cicero says: "Eloquence [*eloquentia*] is nothing else but wisdom delivering copious utterance."[16] Eloquence is to speech what virtue is to human life and thought: "Virtue has a twofold meaning, for it is exhibited either in knowledge or in conduct. The virtue that is designated prudence [*prudentia*] and intelligence and the most impressive name of all, wisdom [*sapientia*], exercises its influence by knowledge alone. . . . The virtue of prudence when displayed in a man's private affairs is usually termed personal sagacity and when in public affairs political widom."[17]

Vico says that "the whole is really the flower of wisdom." He asks, "What is eloquence, in effect, but wisdom ornately and copiously delivered in words appropriate to the common opinion of mankind?"[18] Socrates is often thought to have separated rhetoric or oratory from philosophy. But this is to substitute a view expressed in textbooks of philosophy for what we actually find in Socratic speech. Cicero says: "Socrates was the first to call philosophy down from the heavens and set her in the cities of men and bring her also into their homes and compel her to ask questions about life and morality and things good and evil."[19]

Socrates is the inventor of the philosophical question. Before him the so-called pre-Socratics ask no questions; they simply speak about the nature of things. Socrates is the inventor of philosophical irony, the trope of discursive speech, as well as the elenchus. Cicero says in *Orator* that Socrates "in his discussions separated the science of wise thinking from that of elegant speaking, though in reality they are closely linked together."[20] Cicero says that Socrates is in fact the most eloquent of speakers. He asks: "What of Critias? and Alcibiades? these though not benefactors of their fellow-citizens were undoubtedly learned and eloquent; and did they not owe their training to the discussions of Socrates?"[21]

Socrates is the archetypal figure for the humanist in the comprehension of the triad of *sapientia*, *eloquentia*, and *prudentia*. In the *Republic* Socrates describes the virtues as connected with the body in that they are produced by habits and exercises: "However, the virtue of exercising prudence seems

15. Vico, *New Science*, 157.

16. Cicero, *De partitione oratoria* 23.79.

17. Ibid. 22.76–77.

18. Vico, *Study Methods*, 77–78.

19. Cicero, *Tusculan Disputations* 5.410–11.

20 Cicero, *Orator* 3.16.60.

21. Ibid. 3.34.139; see also 3.32.129.

to belong above all to something more divine, which never loses its power but is either useful and beneficial or useless and harmful, depending on the way it is turned."[22] In the *Republic*, Socrates is always clear that those who best have command of an ability can employ it for right as well as wrong. Thus those who possess the practice of prudence are in a powerful position to turn it into pure cleverness, for prudence, we might say, is a cleverness that is governed by the ideal of the good. This attachment to or love of the good is what separates the tyrannical *psychē* from the philosopher.

We cannot classify Socrates as belonging to either the theoretical or the practical world. All attempts at such classification immediately turn to the opposite. Ernst Cassirer expresses the humanist approach to Socrates when he writes: "As soon as we believe that we have grasped the 'true' face of Socrates and of Socratic thought, then this 'truth' dissolves. Our 'knowledge' is transformed into 'ignorance.' Socrates seems to defy every attempt to 'pin him down'; his every aspect immediately turns into its opposite. This is a fundamental part of Socratic irony. This 'irony' has been borne out again and again in the historical interpretations of the figure of Socrates."[23]

In Plato's early dialogues, Socrates appears as the discoverer of the concept and *logos* as connected to it. He appears, as Cassirer says, as the first great "artist of reason." Sharply opposed to this is Xenophon's picture of Socrates as the moralist and the teacher of prudence. Cassirer sees this as evidence "that the unique problem Socrates poses has not yet been fully understood. This problem consists in the fact that the opposition between theory and practice—the opposition between knowledge and action—has been denied and overcome by Socrates, raising it in a synthesis to a new level. Socrates seems to reject the opposition: for him all knowing is doing."[24]

Socrates raises the problem of the opposition of knowledge and actions to a new level. Cassirer regards the key to this to be the Delphic instruction to "know thyself." He says Socrates "does not call for 'self-knowledge' in the sense of some pure (monadic) looking inward (intro-spection, intuition of the I in the pure act of the *cogito*); instead, it means something completely new and unique for him. This call now means: Know your *work* [*Werk*] and know 'yourself' *in* your work; know what you do, so you can do what you know."[25] *Werk* is the fundamental way in which the self realizes itself. It corresponds to civil wisdom as made by the self acting out of tradition, custom, and culture.

22 Plato, *Republic* 518e.

23. Cassirer, *Metaphysics of Symbolic Forms*, 184.

24. Ibid., 185.

25. Ibid., 185–86.

Giovanni Pico della Mirandola, the great spokesman for the Italian Renaissance humanist tradition, expresses this point by calling attention to the place of self-knowledge in the context of the three Delphic precepts, the third being what he interprets as a theological greeting. Of these three precepts, Pico says: "You will see that they give us no other advice than that we should with all our strength embrace this threefold philosophy." The first is "Nothing too much," which Pico says "prescribes a standard and rule for all the virtues through the doctrine of the Mean, with which moral philosophy duly deals." By citing the "Mean" Pico associates this precept with Aristotle, but it can also be thought to reflect the Socratic interest in moderation or *sophrosynē*. The second is "Know thyself," which Pico says "urges and encourages us to the investigation of all nature, of which the nature of man is both the connecting link and, so to speak the 'mixed bowl.'" Human nature is part of nature, and human beings are thus a "mixed bowl" of the two senses of nature. The third is "Thou art," which Pico claims we come to at the limits of our knowledge of natural philosophy.[26] This third precept is the subject of the famous essay of Plutarch on "The E at Delphi" in the *Moralia*. It is not obvious what the epsilon at Delphi signifies, but the most judicious view is likely that given as the conclusion of Plutarch's essay: "But this much may be said: it appears that as a sort of antithesis to 'Thou art' stands the admonition 'Know thyself,' and then again it seems, in a manner, to be in accord therewith, for the one is an utterance addressed in awe and reverence to the god as existent through all eternity, the other is a reminder to mortal man of his own nature and the weaknesses that beset him."[27]

If prudence is understood as a practical rationality or wisdom, then sagacity or *sapientia*, when taken in combination with it and considered from the humanist perspective, is self-knowledge. The practical rationality that is prudence presupposes a grounding in sagacity or self-knowledge. The self comes to know itself in its productions that are the objective manifestations of itself. Such productions are infused with not only talent but character. Character, as claimed earlier, is built up through habit and the coherence of habits with each other. Character depends upon self-narration. The self must confront its own actions through which it makes its own reality by means of self-narration. This narration must be eloquent in that the self must grasp itself as a whole—a whole that is present in each of its particular moral acts. The effect of this coherence of habits or character is moderation or "nothing too much." The fragmented self is immoderate because it

26. Pico della Mirandola, "Oration," 234–35.
27. Plutarch, *Moralia* 394c.

is perpetually caught in the moment or at least the task at hand, and exists from one act to another without a sense of the whole.

The precept of "thou art" takes us back to the distinction within the whole of wisdom of a knowledge of things human and divine. The idea of the divine as a principle of human existence is that of a limit. Self-knowledge, the self's grasp of its own inner form, if rightly pursued rests on the principle of Socratic ignorance as well as Socratic irony. The self never completely knows itself as a whole because its reality is always in the making. What is beyond the limits of the self's making is the divine, which must simply be acknowledged in a relation of "I am—Thou art." Thus the self is wise only in human things, but this claim necessarily entails a knowledge of the difference between the human and the divine. The divine is not comprehended in terms of its inner form, but it is comprehended as the transcendent that lies beyond the determinate. If the divine is the good, it functions as that which is beyond the virtues as they are reachable within the self as its guides to action, but the good is not itself reachable as an internal relation of the self. The divine good is that to which the self relates itself, but the good itself is in principle what is never fully reachable, but which limits the whole.

The narration by the self of its actions in its realization of its nature, its making of itself, is ironic because the narration never fully captures in words the reality or significance of what is narrated. The self, in its dialectical questioning of itself in its attempt to make its moral character in fact and in word, always fails to attain the whole in a perfect manner. Thus the process of character is always ongoing. The happiness that is the goal of virtuous actions and their comprehension in thought and language is never complete, for the divine good is always beyond full human grasp. Yet the process itself of orienting the human to the divine good is happiness, in the sense of acting in accord with excellence.

PRUDENCE AND JURISPRUDENCE

Prudence is the English translation of the Latin *prudentia*, which is the translation of the Greek *phronēsis*, specifically as it occurs in Aristotle's *Nicomachean Ethics*. In English it can be understood as practical wisdom or practical reason, or even as practical judgment as restricted to the moral sphere. Aristotle says, "prudence is concerned with the human things and with those about which it is possible to deliberate."[28] Prudence is reason as it is involved in choice. Prudence is not the whole of reason because reason has two parts as a human capability: "one part is that by which we

28. Aristotle, *Ethics* 1141b.

contemplate all those sorts of beings whose principles do not admit of being otherwise, one part that by which we contemplate all those things that do admit of being otherwise."[29]

Deliberation is not about the past because "nothing that has come into being is an object of choice. For example, nobody now chooses to have sacked Troy in the past, and nobody deliberates, either, about what has already come into being but rather about what will be and admits of happening."[30] We may contemplate the meaning of what has happened in the past and was once a matter of choice, but our contemplation cannot direct choice to act in such a way that what has happened can be different than it is. But we may employ our contemplation (*theōria*) about the meaning of the past as a basis for our deliberation concerning a matter of choice in the present. Our moral narration, as discussed earlier, brings the past to bear on our current choice. In this sense deliberation is not about the past, but it is grounded in the past. As Aristotle says: "Prudence is necessarily a characteristic accompanied by reason, in possession of the truth, and bound up with action pertaining to the human goods. . . . And since there are two parts of the soul having reason, prudence would be the virtue of one of them, namely, the part involved in the formation of opinions. For both opinion and prudence are concerned with what admits of being otherwise."[31]

There is no science of prudence, for science is concerned with the truth of what is universal: "that prudence is not science is manifest: prudence concerns the ultimate particular thing, as was said, for the action performed is of this kind."[32] It is through particular acts—performed in accordance with the standards of excellence that we set by the virtues—that we aim at happiness. Prudence is necessary for the virtues but the virtues are not in themselves kinds of prudence. Aristotle holds that Socrates "erred when he supposed that all the virtues are kinds of prudence, but he spoke nobly when he said that they do not exist in the absence of prudence. . . . For virtue is not only the characteristic that accords with correct reason, but also the one that is *accompanied* by correct reason. And prudence is correct reason concerning such sorts of things."[33] In his *Commentary on the Nicomachean Ethics* Thomas Aquinas states this point thus: "Socrates erroneously held that all moral virtues are kinds of prudence, since moral virtue and prudence are

29. Ibid. 1139a.
30. Ibid. 1139b.
31. Ibid. 1140b.
32. Ibid. 1142a.
33. Ibid. 1144b.

in different parts of the soul but he was correct in saying that moral virtue cannot be without prudence."[34]

Moral virtue cannot function in the orientation of action toward the good or human happiness without the practice of prudence. The unqualifiedly good person must have a nature in which all the virtues are present. Aristotle says: "It is clear too there will be no correct choice in the absence of prudence, nor in the absence of virtue; for the latter makes one carry out the end, the former the things conducive to the end."[35] Prudence requires not only the presence of virtue but also self-restraint—what Aristotle calls *enkrateia*, literally, inner strength or inner mastery.[36] *Enkrateia* requires mastery over the appetites that lead to excessive pursuit of pleasure as well as excessive spiritedness or rashness of action. In order to practice prudence an inner strength of the self is necessary such that the self can remain steadfast in its perception of the moral, its deliberate choice in response to it, and its course of action. Prudence requires a cleverness on the part of the individual, but prudence cannot be reduced to cleverness in the sense of simply satisfying one's desires or achieving one's own interests.

Kant fails to understand the difference between prudence and cleverness. Once one gives up the standard of excellence that is embodied in the virtues and substitutes for this standard the standard of excellence of the categorical imperative, prudence becomes transformed into an inferior manner of conduct. Prudence becomes an imperfect state, an inferior way of acting that is to be pursued only if the rationality of the decision procedure of the categorical imperative cannot be achieved.

In *Foundations of the Metaphysics of Morals*, Kant makes this clear: "The word 'prudence' [*Klugheit*] may be taken in two senses, and it may bear the name of prudence with reference to things of the world and private prudence. The former sense means the skill of a man in having an influence on others so as to use them for his own purposes. The latter is the ability to unite all these purposes to his own lasting advantage. The worth of the first is finally reduced to the latter, and of one who is prudent in the former sense but not in the latter we might better say that he is clever and cunning [*gescheut und verschlagen*] yet, on the whole, imprudent [*unklug*]."[37] It is no accident that in the *Critique of Judgement* Kant dismisses rhetoric as an improper component of conducting human thought and affairs. Kant says: "*Rhetoric* is the art of transacting a serious business of the understanding as

34. Aquinas, *Commentary*, 602.

35. Aristotle, *Ethics* 1145a.

36. Ibid.

37. Kant, *Metaphysics of Morals*, 33n5.

if it were a free play of the imagination; *poetry* that of conducting a free play of the imagination as if it were a serious business of the understanding."[38] He says further: "Force and elegance of speech (which together constitute rhetoric) belong to fine art; but oratory (*ars oratoria*), being the art of playing for one's own purpose upon the weaknesses of men (let this purpose be ever so good in intention or even in fact) merits no *respect* whatever [*ist gar keiner Achtung würdig*]."[39]

Prudence requires rhetoric or *eloquentia* as the form of speech that allows us to put before ourselves a grasp of the whole. Rhetorical speech is not the speech of the universal imperative but the speech that captures the particular in relation to the whole of the matter of which it is a part. Moral philosophy as grounded in Latinist and humanist thought does not depend upon the application of a logical or categorical principle to a particular instance. Such an application requires an argument to establish that the imperative or principle applies to the instance and to establish how it so applies. But as said earlier, for any argument it is never beyond human wit to devise a counterargument, and such a process has at its center the problem of an indefinite regress of proofs in a process of *ars critica*. A rhetorical approach to moral philosophy and to the deliberation of choice embodies *ars topica*.

Human wit must be applied, not to connect a universal with a particular, but to draw forth from the particular its meaning in relation to virtue and the good. This drawing forth is the product of *ingenium*, of the ability to perceive similarity in dissimilars—to connect particulars together and draw forth their universal meaning. This meaning, then, is present for deliberation in relation to the exercise of choice.

Deliberation requires the art of the Muses, because, in relation to any course of action, we must understand it in terms of what was, is, and is to come. To deliberate is to foretell through contemplation. It is to be able to narrate what is at issue in terms of time, and this requires a grasp of the subject as a whole. Tradition, custom, law, and habit are themselves embodiments of prudence. They are embodiments of practical wisdom that the individual and the society have proven in action over time.

The *Institutes* of Justinian state, "The commandments of the law are these: live honorably; harm nobody; give everyone his due" (*Iuris praecepta sunt haec: honeste vivere, alterum non laedere, suum cuique tribuere*).[40] The jurisprudence of positive law and the habits that form our character from

38. Kant, *Critique of Judgement*, 184.

39. Ibid., 193n.

40. Justinian, *Institutes* 1.1.1.3.

our education and social customs are our guides to human action. When we can act in accordance with these guides, there is no need for deliberation. They provide an eloquence of life that is present at least in traditional societies. Prudence is simply to follow their prudence.

All the art of life is not directed by a knowledge of the jurisprudence of one's nation or even, as Vico would call it, of the "jurisprudence of the human race," which is a knowledge of the actions of providence throughout the world of nations, a knowledge of the principles of their ideal eternal history. The individual, guided by "know thyself" as a principle of his action in the world and by "nothing too much" as a principle of moderation in that action, must take a specific course of life toward goodness and must act in individual occasions that require deliberation. How is prudence in this sense to be learned?

The key to virtuous human action is eloquence. As emphasized, moral goodness is what we tell ourselves after we have acted. The learning of prudence requires us to make a moral act for ourselves in a manner similar to making an intellectual truth for ourselves. The act comes first, but the word is not separate from the act. We act, and the act must then be held in memory. The act must be made into a narration whereby the act can be held in mind as a moral truth. Eloquence is wisdom speaking or putting the whole into words. Every action so held in the memory as a narration is a guide to future action. Memory is the basis of deliberation.

As said earlier, poetry is at the basis of the moral-act-remembered, for the course of the action must be formed as a true story, a *vera narratio*. It must enter the imagination. But the narration must be joined with *ratio*; that is, it must be put into proper arrangement. It must be tested by ingenuity, and the similarities in its dissimilars must be perceived such that the course of action has a necessity of its internal elements. They must be seen as a harmony, grasped in proportion. When we are prompted to deliberate, we find ourselves in the middle of a course of events that has already begun and that is moving on its own toward an end. At the origin there is never need for deliberation.

A set of conditions is born and develops within history toward a point of maturity or crisis, unless it is interrupted from without. The conditions are tied to all the other events affecting them in history. But they have their own history. The point of maturity is potentially the heroic moment of such a course, and it may be naturally dissipated into its future and end. If the course of events in which we find ourselves becomes problematic, it becomes so just past the midpoint, when the course would naturally begin to dissipate and finally find its death among the larger scene of human events.

When events call out for deliberation, we face the problem of the identification of the moral. The moral is an act of seeing. Either we see the presence of the moral or we do not. If we do not see the moral dimension, we may simply become a person. To become a person is to practice the art of overlooking. Every society practices the art of overlooking in that it orders the civil world in a specific way. The vision of the individual is directed by this order, and the problem of good and evil is solved by this order. Society does not engage in dialectics to show itself what has been left out. The individual who identifies the moral and perceives it as counter to the social order has a dialectical vision. The individual sees more than has been seen by society.

The fact that there are other cultures calls every culture into question. But what calls culture into question in ultimate terms is not the fact that there are other cultures, other societies and customs whereby life is actually lived. That there is a way things ultimately are calls any moral state of events into question. Prudence in an ultimate sense is to act in accordance with the way things are, and this is to act absolutely and beyond opposites.

In the *Tao Te Ching* are the lines: "Heaven and Earth are not kind: The ten thousand things are straw dogs to them. Sages are not kind: People are straw dogs to them."[41] The art of the Sage is *wu wei*, "actionless action," which acknowledges that there is a course that anything takes that is natural to it. The problem of prudence in this sense is to remain in accord with it. As with the art of the Muses, one must know the nature of things well enough to act in accordance with them, to foretell. This depends upon memory and eloquence in speech. Argument will not help us, because for every argument there is a counterargument. From this process we can never reach the whole of anything that the deliberation is about.

The passage from the *Tao Te Ching* quoted above ends with the lines: "Longwinded speech is exhausting. Better to stay centered." Argument is endless. Eloquent speech brings things together, as does wisdom. Prudence is eloquence in action. The prudent action, like the perfect word or perfect brush stroke, is completely natural.

Like the action of the Sage, the moral act has an absoluteness about it. Prudence comes into conflict with justice when prudence is understood as simply taking a temperate course of action in order to reduce conflict and opposition. The moral act, if it is truly such, cannot be understood simply as one possible course of action in relation to a given state of affairs. If so, it is a prudent act in the trivial sense of prudence. The intent of the truly moral act is to act in accordance with the good; the good is understood as something

41. *Tao Te Ching*, 5.

beyond opposites. The moral course taken claims to be absolute in relation to what is to be done in this specific case. Justice is the proper harmony or proportion of things, and when the proper harmony has been violated, injustice is perceived. The just man acts in accordance with the good, and no harm can come to a good man.

The distinction made in modern ethics—between *is* and *ought* as the fundamental opposition within which any moral deliberation takes place— ignores the need for a middle term between what is the case and what ought to be the case. In order to pass from one side of this opposition to the other, we must consider what *might* be the case. To do this requires imagination connected to memory. To deliberate and to act in moral terms requires the moral imagination. When the injustice of a given order of things is seen, it must be seen in terms of what can be imagined otherwise. What might be or might have been provides the concrete sense of the possibilities in which the deliberations of practical wisdom can occur.

The self, by acting and narrating to itself the truth of its actions, by placing them under the good, and by formulating these actions in terms of the virtues, develops itself as a theater of communal sense from which it can draw forth the moral places from which to act. This process is like the law, in which the meaning of any case and the presence of any specific law in it, as well as the law itself, are grasped by finding precedents from which to understand the present case.

Prudence is jurisprudence and the converse, in the sense that the moral deliberation of the individual is analogous to that which occurs in the law. As the deliberations in a court of law require not only the presentation of facts and evidence, so these must be placed within a narration such that the whole of the case and its causes can come to light and be grasped by both the imagination and reason. The narration must affect the passions and be vivid, but it must also and at the same time be reasonable. In the circum- stance of individual moral deliberation, the judge and the jury, so to speak, is the individual himself. The judge is his sense of right reason and the jury is his conscience, which, as said earlier, is what keeps the narrative from being simply a rationalization and not a judgment produced by prudence.

FOLLY AND THE MODERN WORLD

The value of the fool, and the importance of folly in human affairs and the light it can throw on prudence, are lost to the modern world and are lost to modern ethics. The loss of folly is the loss of one of the fundamental sources of self-knowledge, but a source of which Renaissance thought was well aware. The fool's authority is folly, and folly is part of nature. The fool is part of human nature. Fools, madmen, and wild men populate the premodern world. The fool in his belled cap, in his feathers, in his rooster suit; the madman with his wild eyes, his nudity, his ability to tolerate extremes of temperature; and the wild man, with his beard and hairy body, sitting in his tree or walking on his hands, peer out at us from their historical place.[42] They greet us around the next corner, at the circus, at the asylum: the insane, giving long lectures to themselves; the wild man of Borneo; the laughing hermit. These are portraits of the human, of its other voices, other rooms. They are here in the walking insane of the cities, in the laughing old coots sitting among their collectibles in a thousand rural landscapes. It is not the hollow wisdom of the mad or the secret knowledge of the wild man that contains instruction of philosophical interest; it is the fool's *folie*.

The urtext in the Western tradition of folly is Sebastian Brant's *Das Narren Schyff*, written in medieval German and published in Basel in 1494. Brant's use of *Narr* as opposed to other terms current at the time (for example, *Tore, Affe, Esel, Gouch*) established it as the primary term for fool. The work contains 112 sections; each, except the last, describes in verse a type of foolishness, and each is prefaced by a woodcut depicting that type of folly. Some of the woodcuts are the work of Albrecht Dürer, who visited Basel between 1492 and 1494.[43] Brant's work was translated into Latin in 1497 by his pupil and protégé Jacob Locher as *Stultifera navis*, which made it available to an international readership. Katherine Anne Porter refers to this translation in her novel *Ship of Fools*.

Although the phrase "ship of fools" is well known, its origins are not. Perhaps some historical remarks on its beginnings are useful. Brant's work became an immediate best seller and was translated into Low German, French, Dutch, Flemish, and English. It was also expanded in various ways. The Flemish thinker Badius Ascensius thought that there were an insufficient number of women on board Brant's ship and wrote an enlarged version with six more ships of female fools (1501).[44] Hieronymus Bosch painted the ship of fools. Erasmus met Brant in 1514 in Strasbourg, and they were probably together again in Antwerp in 1520. Erasmus greatly admired Brant. Brant composed a six-line Latin verse on the appearance of Erasmus's *Moriae encomium* (1509). Hans Holbein furnished illustrations for Erasmus's text in 1514. Erasmus was only eight years younger than Brant, and he was familiar with at least the Latin version of Brant's work before 1509, perhaps through

42. Novak, "Wild Man Comes to Tea."
43. Zeydel, *Sebastian Brant*, 86–87.
44. Doran, *History of Court Fools*, chap. 3.

his friendship with Badius. Brant is the Scholasticist on the threshold of humanism, and Erasmus is the humanist par excellence.

Brant's metaphor of the ship is not original with his work. The idea of putting those living borderline lives in a ship was widespread from Holland to Austria, and the idea of such a ship was the subject of orations, several works, and a sermon before Brant's time.[45] Brant's work, as he himself says at its end, is *gesammlet*, that is, compiled.[46] The title is not original with him and, to a large extent, neither is the content. The portraits of fools are likely built on the practice of the Swabian *fliegende Blätter*, in which flysheets depicting types of fools were circulated with the heading "Der ist ein Narr" ("This is a fool"). Brant's work resembles a collection of such sheets. Like Erasmus, he glosses many biblical passages and classical authors, and his favorite book of the Bible is Ecclesiastes.

The powerful image of the ship of fools has stuck in the Western mind. It may be related to the Roman *carrus navalis* of the festivals of Dionysus-Bacchus, from which comes the word *carnival* and which is connected to the carnival floats in Europe of the sixteenth and seventeenth centuries.[47] But more important for Brant's work is the Christian tradition of the church as the ship of Saint Peter. Jesus embarks on a ship with his disciples (Matt 8:23–27; Mark 4:36–41). Jesus preached from Peter's boat (Luke 5:3). The ship of Christianity is carried over rough seas to heaven. Brant's ship of fools is the inverse of this. It is a vessel of those who have been unable to ingest the wisdom of Christian virtue and who have wasted their substance in the various forms of foolishness that Brant describes. They are on a ship without purpose, unless it be to travel to the underworld. In life they move about aimlessly, with watery souls.

Brant's work is an encyclopedia of folly. He says it is a mirror: "For fools a mirror shall it be, / Where each his counterfeit may see." The mirror will show the truth: "His proper value each would know, / The glass of fools the truth may show." If the mirror reflects when we look in it, then we who see our reflection know we are not wise: "Who sees his image on the page, / May learn to deem himself no sage."[48] Brant says, "One vessel would be far too small, / To carry all the fools I know."[49] The reason for the book is to have "the world's whole course in one brief look."[50] There are

---

45. Brant, *Ship of Fools*, 43.

46. Ibid., 15 and 366.

47. Zijderveld, *Reality in a Looking-Glass*, 77.

48. Brant, *Ship of Fools*, 58.

49. Ibid.

50. Ibid., 59.

"fools galore" in the world, and no one, Brant says, is without the fault of folly in some respect: "Both men and women, all mankind, / Their image in this glass will find."[51] Brant adds, "With caution everyone should look, / To see if he's in this my book."[52]

Brant has produced a foolometer by which we can gauge our own and others' folly. It is a *speculum stultorum*. The forms of foolishness Brant describes range from "Of Useless Books" (those who involve themselves with books in order to glorify themselves but who do not understand the books they have), to "Of Useless Studying" (those who have not learned the proper things: "Thus money spent to train and school / Has often gone to rear a fool"), to "Taking Offense at Fools" (those who ridicule fools or do not heed them, thus quickly becoming fools themselves), to "Blowing into Ears" (those who pass on what others say).[53] In addition to these are the follies we might commonly expect—follies related to envy and hatred, complacency, anger, pride, adultery, bad manners, ingratitude, gambling, contempt of holy writ, making noise in church, causing discord, blasphemy, and so on—and some esoteric follies, such as "Useless Hunting" (spending too much time at it) and "Experience of All Lands" (being overly interested in other places).

The point of Brant's mirror of folly is the recognition of prudence. When we recognize our folly we recognize our need for prudent action. "The Wise Man," his conclusion, is based on the pseudo-Virgilian poem "*Vir bonus*," and his example is Socrates: "A good, wise man of prudence rare, / As one can find scarce anywhere / In all the world, is Socrates."[54] Recognition of folly is the beginning of self-knowledge. This is the ultimate wisdom. Brant says Apollo gave Socrates this gift of prudence.

The key to Socrates' wisdom, for Brant, is his doctrine of ignorance. Nicholas of Cusa, in *De docta ignorantia* (1440), echoes this in his own way by claiming that ignorance is the greatest learning. Cusanus's advice to the searcher for knowledge is parallel to Brant's advice to the searcher for virtue—to find the particular form of folly appropriate to oneself: "Nothing could be more beneficial for even the most zealous searcher for knowledge than his being in fact most learned in that very ignorance which is peculiarly his own; and the better a man will have known his own ignorance, the

51. Ibid., 60.
52. Ibid., 61.
53. Ibid., 125.
54. Ibid., 363.

34

greater his learning will be."[55] The foolish person pretends, to others and to himself, to know how to comport himself—but he does not know.

The key to Socratic wisdom is to know of whatever one knows that there is yet something not known. To be wise in human things is not to be wise in divine things, and human wisdom is above all to know that one is not fully wise in either of them. A doctrine of ignorance is naturally connected with irony (it is ironic that wisdom requires ignorance) and with dialectic (the other side of anything known must always be seen to complete the knowledge of it). A doctrine of ignorance is the key to prudence, for ultimately prudence requires the realization that we do not know what virtue really is. Virtue is always a standard of excellence that we only partially reach, but it is within our reach. We must always think of its opposite; corresponding to every act that seems virtuous is a form of folly, of that act wrongly done.

The teaching of virtue requires example, and it may benefit from the use of images. Brant's use of woodcuts coupled with their embodiment in words is like Shaftesbury's "noble virtuoso scheme of morals."[56] Shaftesbury uses images coupled with commentary to embody this scheme in his unfinished *Second Characters*. Brant's work is less complex than that envisioned by Shaftesbury in that the woodcuts, although quite fine, are not as complex as the emblem of the shield of Hercules or the tablet of Cebes, which Shaftesbury uses and which embody whole fables. The verses that accompany the woodcuts are not extended commentaries, but they combine the image and the word in an allegorical fashion.

The depictions and the verses guide our vision back into the world, to see the folly in human action that otherwise would seem only part of ordinary life. Our vision is heightened in the mirror of Brant's book; we see the world with a new vision, and we see ourselves in it. Like the fool's optics of looking at his scepter, which bears the likeness of a fool, we look and see ourselves in our foolishness. This is the crucial moment for the development of prudence, the sense of things that all virtue requires. Brant intends his book to be a device to affect our vision in the way that the fool actually affects our vision with his mimicking of ordinary actions and words, and although we do not inhabit Brant's world, his forms of folly are mostly still here in our world, if we look.

Erasmus's work is often understood only as satire, as Brant's work is often seen only as a work of Christian moralizing. Erasmus's work is moral satire, but it differs greatly from the satires of manners that appear nearly

---

55. Cusanus, *Learned Ignorance,* 8–9.
56. Shaftesbury, *Life, Unpublished Letters,* 468–69 and 472–74.

one hundred years later, such as *A Horseload of Fools*, by Queen Elizabeth's jester, Tarlton, in which fools go through Fleet Street in a pony cart, or *A Nest of Ninnies, Simply of Themselves Without Compound* (1608), by Shakespeare's fool, Robert Armin. These satires of manners mark the end of the philosophical importance of the fool, who dies at the close of the sixteenth century and is slowly buried in the ages of reason and enlightenment. In the world of method and research there is no place for the fool's impromptu art of inversion. The world ceases to be a theater and becomes a laboratory for the rational and empirical researcher, a shift that culminates in the use of machines as a means of production in the eighteenth century. This world of technology is the subject of chapter 4.

Erasmus thinks differently. His metaphor is the *theatrum mundi*, the theater of the world. It is the stage on which each of us steps to play his role: "What fools these mortals be!" Erasmus says, "Now the whole life of mortal men, what is it but a sort of play, in which various persons make their entrances in various costumes, and each one plays his own part until the director gives him his cue to leave the stage?"[57] He then asks, "What do you think Ecclesiastes meant when he cried out, 'Vanity of vanities, and all is vanity'? No more nor less than this: that all human life is nothing but a stage-play of Folly."[58] The play is at the direction of *Stultitia* or *Moria*, Folly herself, who is the narrator of Erasmus's work. He dedicates his *Moriae encomium* (The praise of folly) to his friend Thomas More, on whose name the title puns; More kept a fool in his household. Since all is folly in Erasmus's account of human affairs, it seems as if the work is a universal satire containing no positive doctrine.

Erasmus says that "the human mind is so constituted that it is far more taken with appearances than reality."[59] If the human comedy is just a comedy in which folly reigns supreme, then all is meaningless. Any meaning found in anything is itself, in truth, just another type of folly. Comedy becomes not an aspect of life but the order of life itself. Erasmus speaks of Momus the mocker.[60] The profession of mockery is a hollow life-form because it requires no self-knowledge, no virtue, and because it can master a situation only by responding to it in a characterless way. A society of mockers is impossible because there is no basis in mockery for any principles of social order. Mockery disturbs folly and its pleasures, Erasmus says. He says that the gods could not tolerate Momus's mockery and threw him out, and "no

---

57. Erasmus, *Praise of Folly*, 43–44.

58. Ibid., 120. See Eccl 1:2 and 12:8.

59. Erasmus, *Praise of Folly*, 71.

60. Ibid., 26–27.

mortal at all deigns to offer him hospitality in his exile."[61] Mockery of folly gives us no insight into its wisdom or its true role in human affairs.

At the beginning of his work Erasmus speaks of "foolosophers," of "foolers" of wisdom and "fool-sages." *Foolosophers* was coined by Sir Thomas Chaloner in the first English translation of Erasmus's work (1549) to play on the Greek word *sophomore* (*sophos*, "wise," *moros*, "foolish"), but inverted as *morosophos*.[62] What is this wisdom? In Brant's work wisdom is the opposite of folly. Yet as I have described it, folly for Brant is the necessary beginning of wisdom; that is, the recognition of folly points toward the need for Socrates' self-knowledge, the key to wisdom in human things. In Brant's terms, recognition is the essential step toward the path of Christian salvation, a place within the ship of Saint Peter instead of the ship of fools. Erasmus sees wisdom within folly itself, not as a goal external to it. The key passage for this in *The Praise of Folly* is that on the fool as the practitioner of "true prudence."[63]

In his attempt to realize the categorical imperative, Kant is on a fool's errand, as are all those since him who have sought ethics in terms of applying theory to practice. To seek a theoretical principle of ethical behavior that can be applied to particular ethical situations is the great fool's errand of modern morals. In morals all is practice; all ethics is "applied," for there is no true theory. Moral life as it is lived is based on analogy: the actions in one instance are guided by those actions accomplished in another. This is what the fool knows, in Erasmus's account, and this is why the fool does not go to books. The fool accepts the particular conditions of life and acts on them.

Prudentia and *providentia* are synonyms in Latin, as they are more or less in English. The prudential, like the providential, is foresight, the ability to see through the situation. This is the fool's art, his folly of wisdom. He takes the events not as fixed but as subject to inversion, to having another nature than they seem to have. The fool is not afraid to act. He acts out of his own innocence, and he prevails because he is not overcome by events. In this way the fool shows us that it is possible to act in any situation. There is no set of events not subject to interpretation in terms of folly and none on which the fool cannot act. When others stand still before a state of affairs, the fool surprises us by the totally unexpected, and movement is shown to be possible. All this is accomplished without a theory, without a full intellectual understanding.

61. Ibid., 26.
62. Ibid., 13n8.
63. Ibid., 42.

As ignorance is a necessary presupposition of our pursuit of wisdom, folly is a recurring presupposition of our pursuit of virtue in action. It is not that the fool is in possession of any particular virtues or of the Good that they embody. The practice of particular virtues in the conscious best life requires reason, yet reason unconnected to folly cannot act in a fully human way. But practical wisdom is not a form of folly. If it were, all would truly be comedy, and life would be truly a comedy of errors, a world of mockery and self-mockery. The fool shows us what it means to act directly out of what one is. He acts as a fool, and the virtuous man, as Aristotle says, must act from a consistent character.

The fool commands a special art of inversion, of acting dialectically, with the power to see to the other side of events that is required for prudence. As mentioned earlier, metaphysics is a guide to morals not because metaphysics offers us experience in theories but because it offers us experience in speculative reason; prudence in this sense is action that allows us to attempt to realize virtue. We discover who we are by seeing ourselves in our actions done in accordance with virtue. Folly, our constant companion, guides us toward happiness, but it is not happiness itself. The positive doctrine of happiness in Erasmus is the happiness of accepting the folly in which we all participate; this requires "decorum," which is crucial to prudence but not equivalent to it.[64] Erasmus's favorite word, *festivus* ("festive," "cheerful," "companionable"), describes the quality that characterizes the good life.

The presence of folly in the world counteracts the objectifying impulse. The struggle in modern thought and in modern life is to come to some form of self-knowledge, civil wisdom, and happiness. Richard Rorty's view in *Philosophy and the Mirror of Nature* is correct that the conception of the mind as the "mirror of nature" has been the guide for the creation of the modern philosopher. As modern philosophy is built the mind is disconnected from human wisdom, and it is disconnected from the divine in order that it be fully connected to the object. The mind ceases to be *nous* or the soul and becomes the Understanding. The concern of the Understanding is not with itself but with the object. The objectifying impulse makes the mind completely worldly. To think is to be objective.

The objectifying impulse is always there in the ancients, the medieval, and the humanists, but the moderns make it their occupation. Freud's discovery of psychoanalysis was immediately controversial because he discovered the self in a world of objective understanding in which the self is conceived only as a cognitive agent. He discovered that inside the self are all the themes that are outside the self in the world of myth and religion and

64. Ibid., 34.

that run beneath all ancient and humanist speculation. The self becomes the subject of the new science of psychoanalysis.

The modern world finally takes its genuine shape. The modern world is composed of psychoanalysis and its variations joined to the cognition of the object. Humanistic thinking, the self in literate discourse with itself, is forgotten, forgotten in the sense that it no longer determines anything in life, except in some individual lives. Rorty looks into the mirror of nature and sees the disappearance of the humanist and eighteenth-century wit. He proposes "conversation," the humanist stock-in-trade.[65] It is too little, too late.

The objectifying impulse leads finally to the barbarism of reflection. Reflection presents the object as a vacuous actuality, that is to say, as a given that has no inner life or significance. Both the phenomenal object and the thing-in-itself are vacuous givens, since their significance lies only in the role they play in the activity of judgment. The self cannot be reached by the employment of concepts unless it is reached simply as another object or given. The self of the behavioral sciences and cognitive psychology or cognitive science is the self as an object investigated by reflective understanding. It is the self as here and now, functioning in the world. This is true even if attention is directed to the self's use of metaphors or tropes of various sorts to define this world. The self of the humanist is not reducible to such study.

The speculative impulse runs counter to the objectifying impulse and upsets the order of the world accessible to the concept joined to the sense perception. The first form in which the self encounters itself as subject rather than as object is the act of inversion. Inversion is rooted in the passion of wonder. The capacity for wonder allows us to experience the object as a marvel, as marvelous. The marvel as something before the mind is never fully seen even by the mind's own eye. The marvel breaks into time and brings with it a glimpse of the beyond. Anton Zijderveld says, "Folly is very much an aboriginal layer of consciousness in the human species, testifying to impulses which lay, as it were, prior to any socializing and civilizing process, piercing through the veneers of culture with an unpredictable, often noisy and irritating force."[66]

The marvel reached by the capacity of wonder appears at the point dividing the human and the divine. What is marvelous is always touched with the miraculous. The fable, *fabula*, is rooted in the power of speech to narrate or form what is seen as a true story. To form the seen as a story is to understand it as having a beginning, middle, and end. The reality grasped in

65. Rorty, *Mirror of Nature*, esp. 389–94.
66. Zijderveld, *Reality in a Looking-Glass*, 77.

the narration of these three moments, which are identical with the original powers attributed to the Muses (to tell us of what was, is, and is to come), is not vacuous. What is fabulous, the marvelous, has an inner life. The self exists in the process of birth, maturity, and death, and a fable that illuminates these moments in their interconnections offers the self a way to grasp its own being. The world is full of the fable: the stories parents tell to children, the stories families tell to themselves, the life stories of individuals, the histories of nations, the stories of the gods and of the actions of the divine in the world.

At the basis of the speculative, the fabulous, the marvelous, is the phenomenon of inversion. Not all fables or marvels are directly about inversion, although inversion is a subject that should always be investigated by the philosophers. The power to invert the world lets the self know it exists. Inversion is its own unique power that can produce the laugh, that can establish the divine as an order beyond the rational order formed by the Understanding. To invert what is there before us lets us know that we are. The inversion is a wonder; we are stopped before it.

Inversion of events need not be the extreme inversion to the logical opposite. The inversion may be only to point ironically to a different order of meaning. The poet and the true philosopher know this, and their productions are based on the capacity for wonder that the possibility of world-inversion engenders. The poet and philosopher stand common sense on its head and oppose literal-mindedness. Their activity shows this power of the marvelous to the mind in words. In this sense their speech can be thought mad, because it is a speech that is between the purely human and the divine.

The fool differs from the poet and philosopher in that the fool shows such truth directly in the world in actions and in his very presence, in his motley and belled cap. His words and his actions overtly break into consciousness and into the fabric of society. His thoughts are not the same as those of the poet and the philosopher. Yet all three are tied to wisdom, for the poet imitates what the philosopher pursues in reason, and the fool's inversion is a key to prudence. The fool always teaches us something; we can never tell quite what.

The poet and the philosopher are followers of the Muses, who are presided over by Mnemosyne, or Memory, the mother of the Muses. The fool and those of us who have gone to school with the masters of folly know that the Feast of Fools is a scene of our humanity. The *sottie*, the Feast of Fools, is presided over by Mère-Folle. She is the mother of this brood of sots, knaves, and ninnies, and she alternately nurtures and mocks them. Mère-Folle is Erasmus's Moria, who specializes in foolosophy and reminds us that the bacchanalian revel constantly inverts itself. Mnemosyne and Mère-Folle are the mothers of us all. The question is how to live with them. In the barbarism of reflection of the technological society, folly remains, but it remains denied and unnoticed. If we can remember even some of what folly is, we may gain a vital standpoint outside the modern order. This memory can allow us to transcend the dominance of the Understanding and grasp the dialectical power of speculative reason and its connection with true prudence.

Speculation and prudence, the topics opened up by the fool, come together through the exercise of philosophical memory. Once the barbarism of reflection takes its full form as technological society, philosophy is left helpless to be more than reflective and ratiocinative; it must limit itself to the powers of the Understanding as opposed to the broader powers of Reason to speak of the whole. Only when philosophy remembers its original connection to memory and to poetic and rhetoric can it project another version of itself in the modern world. Speculative reason becomes the one agency that acts against the destruction of memory in the building of the technological order. Technology and philosophy then find themselves in a dialectical struggle with each other, a struggle that has no immediate resolution. If philosophy engages in this struggle, instead of merging its own form with that of technology, it finds a new place to stand. This new place is the revival of the energies and insights of its origin in self-knowledge.

THE CARDINAL VIRTUES

"Cardinal" is from the Latin term *cardo*, "hinge," which in its transferred meaning is that on which everything else hinges or depends, the chief point or circumstance or consideration upon which many others depend. We can speak of the *quattuor cardines mundi*, the four cardinal points or directions. The four cardinal virtues that come to us from Plato and Aristotle are wisdom (*sophia*), courage (*andreia*), moderation (*sōphrosynē*), and justice (*dikaiosynē*). These are the chief virtues, the excellences to which we can aspire to govern our conduct as human beings, that Plato presents in Book 4 of the *Republic* and Aristotle enumerates in Book 2 of the *Nicomachean Ethics* along with other virtues—such as liberality, magnificence, and friendliness—which are discussed throughout the work.

My concern is with the cardinal virtues, for when they are present the more specific virtues follow and, to an extent, are even versions of the cardinal. It is through the cardinal virtues that the good (*agathos*) and happiness or well-being (*eudaimonia*) is to be reached, although the virtues are not to be equated with such. Like the cardinal points of north, south, east, and west, by which we orient ourselves in the visible world, the cardinal virtues

41

of wisdom, courage, moderation, and justice are the standards by which the mind's eye orients the soul toward the good and human happiness. This orientation of the soul is all but lost in the modern world of the ideologies of political correctness, diversity, entitlement, and the second chance and has disappeared from the moral philosophy of the categorical imperative, the utility of the greatest number, and the aggregate of issues of applied ethics. Let us bring back from memory something of the nobility of these great virtues, not as a strict interpretation of their meanings in Greek philosophy but as how they might simply be seen as part of common life and moral philosophy that is connected to it.

Wisdom (*sophia* or *sapientia* as distinguished from *phronēsis* or *prudentia*) is the object of philosophy, and, as discussed earlier, at the center of philosophy is the pursuit of self-knowledge. Wisdom is an excellence of the mind, not of the body. The other three cardinal virtues involve the body. There is no disembodied human thought, but thought as contemplation is a power exercised apart from the body. The love of wisdom is not the love of body. The pleasure of contemplation is not the object of contemplation, but it is one of its benefits and is essentially a pleasure of mental activity, which only secondarily may have the bodily effects of tranquility of the passions and the appetites. Wisdom aims at a grasp of the whole of experience. In this respect wisdom differs from knowledge. Knowledge is partial. It looks to the various aspects of experience that constitute fields of knowledge, but there is no "field" of wisdom set off against other fields of knowledge or cognition. To contemplate is to look to the whole of things and to attempt by theoretical reason to comprehend their nature in themselves and in their ultimate relations to each other. Such activity of the mind is pursued apart from the connection of thought with action. When thought is directed to action, reason becomes practical; it practices prudence.

What is the connection between wisdom as *sophia* and even contemplation as *theoria* and *phronēsis* or prudence? None of the virtues can be pursued apart from prudence, but prudence is not a power *sui generis*. To conceive prudence as a power *sui generis* is simply to cast the relation of thought and action in terms of a deontological principle such as the categorical imperative or utility. Practical reason depends upon reason, and reason exercised apart from action but directed to experience is a pursuit of wisdom. To attempt to think of the whole of experience is to think metaphysically and ontologically. Metaphysics is the source for moral philosophy; that is, it is often characterized in ethics as the ultimate standard to which we may appeal in a dispute between two views of the solution to a moral problem.

An ethical dispute is said to become a dispute finally between two metaphysical views of the world. This offers no resolution because there is no known way to resolve such a dispute; it is the same as if one has an argument and counterargument—an antinomy. Instead, metaphysical thought provides experience in a holistic manner of comprehension that can be applied to grasp a given moral circumstance about which we deliberate as its own whole—to regard it in terms of its past, present, and future and thus orient judgment to produce choice. Furthermore, the metaphysical pursuit of the True as the whole involves that the whole is a limit, a thing in itself. This sense of the limit when connected to the moral appears as the good. The metaphysics of experience when it faces the limit of experience becomes an ontology, because *ontos* or being itself is the one that is transcendent of the many within experience. In moral terms the being of ontology corresponds to the good. Thought connects to action through prudence, which governs the attainment of the virtues. But the good is not the sum total of the pantheon of virtues; the good is that to which they each refer.

The good life is more than simply the life of virtue, even though it requires virtue. Happiness or well-being, *eudaimonia*, requires practical reason or prudence to lead the moral individual to the peace of reason. The peace of reason is the kind of detachment that is represented by Socrates and Socratic philosophy. The good life or best life, although engaged in the exercise of the virtues in regard to specific moral actions, is one in which the individual makes no one the worse for knowing him. This standpoint is analogous to the advice of the Hippocratic oath—that the physician should first do no harm. We seek the good or best life because we are mortal. Our mortality is the cause of our morality. We cannot do better than to adopt the Socratic maxim that no harm can come to a good individual. Our natural inclination to happiness takes the path of the cultivation of the virtues, and they give our happiness positive content, but ultimately our happiness depends upon what we do not do as a matter of choice—to make no one the worse for knowing us. Our genius in this regard, our good daimon, is our mastery over the passions and the appetites and our attunement of our reason with the perspective of the whole. This attunement is self-knowledge as it guides conduct and confronts the human fact of mortality.

The principle that the True is the whole is compatible with the doctrine of Socratic ignorance. The wisdom of the thought of the whole is also an ignorance of the whole; the whole itself can never be realized in thought because thought can approach the whole only from within the whole. This metaphysical truth corresponds to the moral truth that the good is not fully reachable in any given action or formulation of moral character. We remain ignorant of the good in itself and can only assert it in the prohibition of doing no harm to others and the necessary belief that no harm can come to a good human being. But to hold these assertions is evidence of happiness because they require the self-possession that depends upon self-knowledge.

Courage in its Greek meaning (*andreia*), as related to the noun *anēr*, a male human being, connotes "manliness." I intend this cardinal virtue more broadly in the sense of "fortitude," from Latin *fortitudo*, having the sense of strength of mind that enables one to endure physical pain or mental and emotional adversity with courage. I intend courage not simply as the ability to endure such circumstances but as the active power to face danger or great difficulty involving one's well-being with self-possession, confidence, resolution, and bravery (connected to Latin *cor*, "heart"). As wisdom is an excellence of the mind, courage is an excellence of the heart or spirit of an individual. A man or woman can be spoken of as courageous in two senses: as someone who is able to face a physical danger with self-possession and resolution, and as someone who is able to confront political power that would conduce the person to a reduction of human dignity and loss of rightful place. Courage, then, is strength of character and spirit in the face of serious adversity involving the risk of life and limb or of livelihood and lively selfhood.

Courage is a mean that falls between recklessness and cowardice. The courage of the warrior that is discussed in chapter 2 is not recklessness or fearlessness but the risk of self-sacrifice for the sake of a moral ideal. Courage involves a purpose that has moral significance that is larger than simply the individual's self-interest, although it may take courage simply to save oneself in a given circumstance, and this too should be recognized as courage. But an act of courage as a truly virtuous act involves willful and deliberate choice. Cowardice need not invoke flight from a threat; it may be simply the willingness to accept a reduction of one's selfhood and human dignity, a submission to unjustified power. But what might appear as cowardly submission to power might not actually be such. It might actually be courage delayed—an avoidance of reckless self-sacrifice that might appear dramatically commendable at the moment, but ineffective. Real prudence of courage might require the cleverness of submission that creates conditions for future success. Such prudence acts in accordance with the logic of the Trojan horse and requires the wisdom of the whole.

Moderation or temperance, *sōphrosynē*, in a limited sense and the sense prominent in Aristotle's ethics, is the direction or modification of bodily desires and pleasures. It certainly can have this meaning, standing between licentiousness and asceticism. The Delphic precept of "nothing too much" or moderation in all things can be taken in this sense—that a proper life requires a balance between bodily pleasures and mental and spiritual pleasures, between the animal and the rational in the human being. *Sōphrosynē*, then, is an inner harmony of the human. But in a wider and perhaps more Platonic sense, *sōphrosynē* is a state of the soul, an excellence of conduct in relation to others.

Above all, *sōphrosynē* is a counter to arrogance. Arrogance is the result of being overly convinced of one's own importance: "arrogate," to claim or assume for oneself without right (Latin *arrogare*). Moderation or *sōphrosynē* is a mean in this sense between undue timidity of soul and arrogance. Timidity of soul is to a large degree harmless unless it engenders a level of inaction when action is required, so that it is a detriment to the welfare of others. Then it is a kind of cowardice. Arrogance seems the more serious extreme, as it is an aggressive form of false excellence.

Arrogance is a corruption of the psyche. Arrogance is dangerous because it is not tempered by any sense of ignorance. The arrogant person possesses the truth and the right way with no need to justify them. Arrogant thought is impervious to the Socratic question and borders on the personality of the psycho-sociopath discussed in chapter 3. In politics the arrogant are prone to ideology. Moderation as a virtue is achieved by the principle of Socratic ignorance embodied in the Socratic question. To be moderate in thought and action is to be open to correction and alteration. A moderate course of thought and action is firm, but it conceives others as partners. The arrogant person is antihuman, a great nuisance and an unpleasant presence.

Justice is the center of Plato's *Republic* and the focus of the fifth book of Aristotle's *Nicomachean Ethics*, and it is characterized in Cicero's *De officiis* as "the crowning glory of the virtues and on the basis of which men are called 'good men.'"[67] For Plato a just man and a just state require a harmony among the parts of the soul and the classes of the state such that each part is given its due in proportion to the others. For Aristotle justice is the right relation between persons, as given in the law. He says, "This justice, then, is complete [or perfect (*teleios*)] virtue, though not unqualifiedly but in relation to another person. And on account of this, justice is often held to be the greatest of the virtues, neither the evening star nor the morning dawn being so wonderous."[68]

Justice and just action require making distinctions as found in law. All are equal under the law as persons, but this universal standard of equality does not mean what is today known as "social justice." The advocates of social justice take the law into their own hands and identify justice with the view of human society that they hold. In this way they become lawgivers

67. Cicero, *De officiis* 1.7.20.
68. Aristotle, *Ethics* 1129b.

without the wisdom of Solon, for they are guided not by the Delphic precepts but by their own feelings, which masquerade as thoughts. In the concept of social justice, justice ceases to be a transcendental standard to which any form of social order must be accountable. The classic relation of society to justice is inverted such that what justice is, is answerable to whatever the social is deemed rightly to be. All becomes politics and politics becomes governed by mass feelings or by those who claim to speak for them. In the concept of social justice, justice is not a virtue; it is a politics.

To call justice back to its status as a virtue requires a change of mind in which truth and the True stand outside history, as does the good, for justice is the good in human affairs. In these affairs justice is based upon making distinctions among individuals according to their merits and their stations and their duties. The politically correct concept of social justice advocates an ideology embodied in the metaphor of an "equal playing field." This view rests on the idea of entitlement—namely, that individuals who have attained particular status or wealth in society are simply more fortunate and that social justice requires that the position of such individuals be modified such that the gap between the "less fortunate" and the "more fortunate" can be lessened or, ideally, closed. Justice is not conceived as an objective standard of equality, but as the notion that all persons are entitled to a certain level of social and economic existence without regard to their contribution to the social order or economic success.

Eliminated in the equal playing field ideology is freedom as self-determination. Determination of the individual's circumstances is in the hands of the social collective. Social justice is a modern version of Thrasymachus's definition of justice in the *Republic*—that justice is whatever the stronger determines it to be, and in this case the stronger is the power that underlies the ideology of social justice.

Justice understood as a virtue of human conduct is excellence in affording each individual or circumstance its proper right, its due. Justice is the virtue closest to the good, for just action toward anything is taken in terms of what is good for the thing. Justice is the virtue that holds all the virtues in proper proportion to each other.

We cultivate the cardinal virtues as well as the others, not for their own sake but in order to have a good life. We aim at the good because only a good person can be happy. Happiness or well-being is the presence of the good in human life. But what is happiness? Happiness is not continual good feeling about things, because the good life is a tragicomic event involving misfortune and fortune. Happiness is the result of good character that carries us through. We pursue happiness because we are mortal. Happiness does not designate a particular state of mind that we achieve from time to time; it properly refers to a condition achieved over a complete life. Only when the complete speech of a person's life can be given, can it be said to have been a happy life.

Happiness is without question tied to pleasure. Aristotle says, "all people suppose the happy life to be pleasant, and they weave pleasure into happiness—reasonably so. For no activity is complete when it is impeded, but happiness is among the things that are complete." We cannot imagine happiness or a happy life as unpleasant, even though the happy person must endure what is often unpleasant and painful. Aristotle says further, "the happy person needs in addition the goods residing in the body as well as external goods and chance, so that he not be impeded in these respects."[69] Happiness requires a reasonably good level of bodily health. To exist in a continual state of insufferable pain is an impediment to any achievement of human happiness.

Cicero says that the only cure for insufferable pain is death.[70] In addition, happiness requires for its possibility that one have money and the means to support oneself. An existence of abject, unrelieved poverty prevents one from pursuing happiness. Furthermore, one needs chance or good fortune; that is, happiness requires some luck—that some things come one's way and that one does not constantly struggle with adversity. This sense of chance is incorporated for Aristotle in *eudaimonia*, in the idea of having a good daimon.

Although happiness incorporates pleasure, pleasure is not the sole principle of happiness. More than the pursuit of pleasure and avoidance of pain is necessary for the pursuit of happiness. Pleasure is not self-sustaining; one instance of pleasure requires another, and so on. Pleasure does not fully engage the spirit. Thus one might turn to the pursuit of honor as the means to happiness. Honor satisfies the claims of spirit, but it contains the same problem of transitoriness as pleasure. For an honor, once achieved, is most luminous when first bestowed and later can become the basis for further honors. Honors are always relative to certain conditions, and conditions eventually change. Honor is rooted in the sociality of human life.

Also so rooted is friendship. Happiness does not require honor but it does require friends. Aristotle says, "For friendship is a certain virtue or is accompanied by virtue; and, further, it is most necessary with a view to life: without friends, no one would choose to live, even if he possessed all other goods."[71] To be human and to have a good life, one needs friends in the

---

69. Ibid. 1153b.

70. Cicero, *Tusculan Disputations* 2.66–67.

71. Aristotle, *Ethics* 1155a.

sense of others who recognize the value of each other. To be human is to be social and to have recognition by others.

If the above factors are necessary conditions for happiness, what is the necessary and sufficient condition for happiness—that without which happiness is at best partial and incomplete? Given that one can live life in ordinary terms without fundamental impediments to happiness, happiness is finally tied to contemplation.

Wisdom is an intellectual virtue, an excellence of mind that is not the same as contemplation. As described earlier, wisdom is the ability to grasp a situation as a whole and to comprehend its past, present, and future. Such comprehension can direct prudence, which can bring such wisdom as well as other virtues to bear on conduct in relation to a situation. Contemplation is a state of continual thoughtfulness, a state of sustained attention to the nature of things. It is speculative thinking that is generated by the sense of wonder. It entails the pleasure of detachment and self-determination, a holding of one's place in the midst of things. Contemplation is mental freedom. It is what in ordinary discourse is often referred to as a "philosophic approach to life." Human happiness ultimately requires mastering the fear of death. This mastery cannot be had by the pursuit of pleasure, wealth, or honor because they are tied to the body and its passions. It is through contemplation that we can arrive at the consolation of the Socratic maxim that no harm can come to a good person, and one becomes good through character formed by the pursuit of the virtues.

DECORUM, DUTY, AND DIGNITY

For Cicero the four cardinal virtues come together in what can be called, in Latin, *decorum* or propriety. Of decorum or propriety Cicero says, "Such is its essential nature, that it is inseparable from moral goodness; for what is proper is morally right, and what is morally right is proper." Morality is not identical with propriety because morality is a somewhat wider sense of right conduct that propriety embodies. Decorum or propriety is something that cannot be taught by any critical method of reasoning. It comes from human beings' activity in any situation in terms of human dignity. It is a sense of the civil applied in life and brought forth from it. Cicero continues, "The nature of the difference between morality and propriety can be more easily felt than expressed. For whatever propriety may be, it is manifested only when there a pre-existing moral rectitude."[72]

72. Cicero, *De officiis* 1.27.93–94.

Cicero says, "This propriety, therefore, of which I am speaking belongs to each division of moral rectitude; and its relation to the cardinal virtues is so close, that it is perfectly self-evident and does not require any abstruse process of reasoning to see it."[73] The propriety we seek is that which "we may infer from that propriety which poets aim to secure. . . . Now, we say that the poets observe propriety, when every action is in accord with each individual character."[74] Propriety involves considerateness, self-control, and moderation in all things and as such it gives a sort of polish to life. This polish, as will be evident later, is a property of human dignity. Cicero says, "For to employ reason and speech rationally, to do with careful consideration whatever one does, and in everything to discern the truth and to uphold it—that is proper."[75] The humanist ideal of "wisdom speaking" discussed earlier is rooted in propriety, because prudent action that follows from sapience and eloquence is proper. Prudent action is just. Furthermore, Cicero holds, "If there is any such thing as propriety at all, it can be nothing more than uniform consistency in the course of our life as a whole and all its individual actions."[76]

Cicero says, "We conclude that the duties prescribed by justice must be given precedence over the pursuit of knowledge and the duties imposed by it; for the former concern the welfare of our fellow-men; and nothing ought to be more sacred in men's eyes than that."[77] Propriety is a kind of duty that is allied most highly with justice. It is not a duty derived from the categorical imperative, although considerateness would accord with the principle of treating others as ends and not as means. As a duty, propriety or decorum is not a duty in respect of some specific obligation. Propriety is a duty to uphold the dignity of the human being as a social animal, a duty to fulfill what the human itself is. The centrality of propriety for morality stems from a view of life that contrasts to that of utilitarianism.

John Stuart Mill states that particular issues that may be raised concerning the nature of pleasure and pain and the standard by which to explain them do not affect "the theory of life on which this theory of morality [utilitarianism] is grounded—namely, that pleasure and freedom from pain are the only things desirable as ends."[78] The motivation to propriety in human action is not comprehensible as a drive toward pleasure and an

---

73. Ibid. 1.27.95.
74. Ibid. 1.28.97.
75. Ibid. 1.27.94.
76. Ibid. 1.31.111.
77. Ibid. 1.43.155.
78. Mill, *Utilitarianism*, 10.

avoidance of pain. We might claim that to pursue propriety is a form of the pursuit of pleasure—that propriety is pleasurable—but this would suggest that whatever is positive in human affairs is pleasure. But then, what is pleasure? Pleasure may be either mental or physical or a combination of both, but it is not a virtue; it is a desirable condition of human existence, but it is not an excellence of the soul.

Cicero endorses three principles for the duty of propriety: "first, that impulse shall obey reason; for there is no better way than this to secure the observance of duties."[79] If we ask in this regard for an explanation of what constitutes reason, holding that all reason is relative, a kind of subjugation of reason in human affairs to politics, we will find a counter to such in the adherence to reason in the law. Jurors are asked to apply reason to reach a verdict, and if the verdict is "guilty," it must be beyond a reasonable doubt. Reason when called on allows law to function and, in like manner, reason can simply be affirmed in matters of morality. Character is formed through the use of reason to control impulse, as discussed earlier.

Cicero's second principle is "that we estimate carefully the importance of the object that we wish to accomplish, so that neither more nor less care and attention may be expended upon it than the case requires."[80] This is a rule that can be connected to prudence in the sense that prudence is an effective manner of moral action, not simply a manifestation of an ideal or the taking of a stand simply "on principle." Cicero says, "the third principle is that we be careful to observe moderation in all that is essential to the outward appearance and dignity of a proper person."[81] It is important for the success of an action not only that it be what it is as an instance of moral rectitude but also that it appear to be so. Society depends upon recognition of what is proper, and the individual has a duty to attempt not only to act with propriety but, in addition, to attempt in so doing to further the sense of propriety among others by setting an example.

Cicero concludes, "of these three principles, the one of prime importance is to keep impulse subservient to reason."[82] Propriety or decorum, then, is above all the presence of reason in human affairs. It is a duty to be fully and uniquely human—to be dignified.

The classic treatment of human dignity in the humanist tradition, as cited earlier, is Pico's "Oration on the Dignity of Man," which was written to serve as a preface to the nine hundred philosophical theses Pico intended to

---

79. Cicero, *De officiis* 1.39.141.

80. Ibid.

81. Ibid.

82. Ibid.

debate. The "Oration" has come to stand on its own. Pico's aim is to extol the unique worth of the human being within the being and beings of the world. His project in this brief account recalls the Greek *axia* (related to axiom or *axion*), which can mean both worthiness and merit—what is rightly deserved. It is related to the verb *axioun*—to deem oneself worthy. Pico wishes to express the worth or merit of the human in the natural order of things. Man can engage in rightful self-praise because there is no other creature that is the maker of its own nature. Man makes his own nature from the divine endowment of human nature.

Pico says, "At last the best of artisans ordained that that creature to whom He had been able to give nothing proper to himself should have joint possession of whatever had been peculiar to each of the different kinds of being. He therefore took man as a creature of indeterminate nature and, assigning him a place in the middle of the world, addressed him thus. . . . We have set thee at the world's center that thou mayest from thence more easily observe whatever is in the world."[83] Thus man does not make human nature but man makes the distinctively human world as an extension of his divinely begotten nature. Man is the only animal that takes its own nature as an object of knowledge, the only animal that engages in self-knowledge.

Pico's praise of human dignity is reinforced by the "Fable about Man" of the Spanish humanist Juan Luis Vives. In contrast to the Scholastic definition of man in terms of rationality, Vives begins his brief "Fable" with the assertion that man is a fable (*fabula*) and a play (*ludus*).[84] This assertion may call attention to Aristotle's claim in the *Poetics* that man is the only animal that is mimetic, that imitates. In Vives' fable, Jupiter has arranged a banquet, followed by an entertainment, to honor Juno on her birthday. As part of this entertainment man plays various roles, first imitating a plant and an animal. He then plays a human being, then a god, and finally imitates Jupiter himself—all to the great delight of the pantheon of gods who are guests at the evening. The gods are so impressed by man that they invite him to come and sit with them in their gallery.

Man appears as a marvel, a creature that can make himself into any other in the order of nature. Animals do not have the ability of *mimēsis*, nor do gods. Gods can change the identity through which they appear, but they do not imitate. They do not have the power of the mask, whereas man does. Man can make himself into a fable and act it out as if it were real. Man has the power to play any role for any purpose at will.

83. Pico della Mirandola, "Oration," 224–25.

84. Vives, "Fable," 387.

The power to play a role is the basis of human freedom, understood as the power of self-determination. Moral freedom is self-determination in terms of the standard of excellence set by the virtues that lead to human happiness. Vives says, "then, as he of gods the greatest, embracing all things in his might, is all things, he saw man, Jupiter's mime, be all things also."[85]

Fundamental to the human is *poiēsis*, making or producing in general, and the composing of poetry as a form of making (*poiein*). Man makes his being through his roles. The humanist doctrine of human role-playing may seem to deny the conception of a human nature, but it does not. On the humanist view the nature of man is mimetic; man makes his nature through his culture, which is a second nature that overlies the natural world. Culture is human nature writ large. The fact that man can make himself is the necessary condition for man to make himself as a moral being.

Morality is a particular role the human being can play, and this role is dependent on the ability to narrate one's actions in terms of the standards of the virtues. The habits so formed and the comprehension of them in rational narration of their meaning and justification make character. We become our moral selves through the power to assume the role of moral actor in the theater of the world, in which all possible human roles, all versions of the human, exist.

Giambattista Vico has expressed this conception of making in his principle of *verum esse ipsum factum*, or *verum et factum convertuntur*—the true is the same as the made, convertible with the made.[86] This is the principle that underlies the human world as such. Man makes history but man does not make his own nature, in Vico's view. Man's nature is divinely begotten. It is from this nature that the true is made. This principle is not a version of historicism, because history is governed by the providential order of *corso* and *ricorso* of human events. Prudence and providence are synonyms. As things repeat themselves generally in history, so things repeat themselves in particular circumstances. Because of this eternal pattern of repetition prudence is possible, and in fact is necessary, in the making of the moral judgments and actions that generate and maintain us as moral beings.

The theater of the world is Socrates' stage on which the moral roles can be observed and questioned. Morality and moral philosophy must always return to Socrates—the first to ask moral questions in pursuit of the Delphic precepts. As Vico claims, "Doctrines must take their beginning from that of the matters of which they treat."[87] In James Joyce's *Ulysses*, Stephen

85. Ibid., 389.

86. Vico, *Ancient Wisdom*, 46.

87. Vico, *New Science*, 92.

remarks, "Maeterlink says: *If Socrates leave his house today he will find the sage seated on his doorstep. If Judas go forth tonight it is to Judas his steps will tend.* Every life is many days, day after day. We walk through ourselves, meeting robbers, ghosts, giants, old men, young men, wives, widows, brothers-in-love, but always meeting ourselves."[88] In *Finnegans Wake* we find this: "As who has come returns."[89] The theater of the world is governed by memory—what is, always was before—and to comprehend what is we must turn to what it was before.

The decisive objection to my tetralogy of modern moral vices—political correctness, diversity, entitlement, and the "right" to a second chance—is that they are undignified. They rob the citizens of societies that are so dominated of the dignity that is rightfully theirs as human individuals. In his account of the passions from which society originates, Vico places deep fear (*spavento*) and shame or modesty (*pudore*) as fundamental. These two passions are not found among animals, and they are what make the human being distinctively human.[90] The fear of which Vico speaks is not pragmatic fear, that is, fear associated with some particular danger; it is existential fear, the fear human beings feel at being in the world—that they do not own existence or the conditions of life in general. Shame or modesty is not felt in animals, although domestic animals can be shamed and conditioned to have a shameful response. The human feeling of modesty and the shame that accompanies immodesty is the basis of decorum in human action. It is at the basis of our sociability with others. Modesty is our awareness that our existence requires particular comportment with others. It is the root of civil wisdom, our motivation to be members of the polis.

In addition to these two passions Vico speaks of curiosity.[91] He intends curiosity in the sense of interest leading to inquiry. Curiosity is the passion that underlies and motivates ingenuity (*ingenium*), the ability to see similarity in dissimilars, and that in its most profound sense leads to wonder. Fear, shame, and curiosity are not virtues but passions that lie at the basis of the human. We can say of them, as Aristotle says specifically of shame, "it is not fitting to speak about a sense of shame as a particular virtue, for it seems more like a passion than a characteristic. It is defined, at any rate, as a certain fear of disrepute, and it turns out to resemble the fear of terrible things, for those who feel shame blush and those who fear death turn pale."[92]

88 Joyce, *Ulysses*, 175.

89. Joyce, *Finnegans Wake*, 296.

90. Vico, *New Science*, 173–78.

91. Ibid., 71 and 118.

92. Aristotle, *Ethics* 1128b.

In modern technological society, as discussed in chapter 4, life becomes fearless, shameless, and bereft of the need for curiosity. Modern persons are fearless, feeling that we live in a world of certainty or potential certainty in which all problems can be conquered by the perfection of technology; shameless, because we have no need of private lives—anything that is in fact personal may be publicly said or done; bereft of curiosity, because all problems are a matter of methodological procedure—we are surrounded by therapies and services for the solution of all human problems.

In modern technological society the person has no moral worth, no dignity, because the value of individual judgment is diminished, even eliminated. No one is encouraged to be eccentric. The doctrines of political correctness, diversity, entitlement, and the second chance make the individual a functionary. These doctrines and the social programs connected to them are fearless and shameless in their demands on individual dignity. Where there is constant talk of individuality, there is no regard for its reality. Curiosity is unnecessary and unwanted because the ideologies embodied in such doctrines leave no open questions. All is settled by the practices of administrated life. Dignity requires the Socratic sense of the gadfly and independent insight derived from the attachment to virtue and the freedom of self-determination generated by the pursuit of self-knowledge.

Neither the ethics of the categorical imperative—act such that one's actions could become a universal law—nor the ethics of utility of the greatest good for the greatest number offers a basis for the development of dignity. A decision procedure, which both provide, offers a basis for moral judgment with the accompanying problems of how this judgment can be properly guided, but the production of such judgments does not result in a ground for human dignity. Dignity depends upon the development of character. Expertise in moral judgment is desirable in morality, but it is not character. Character is the essence of the whole person built up through virtue and the attempt to attain the good life. Dignity does not result from the application of theoretical principles to a moral situation.

All morality is applied, but not in the manner of connecting principles to particulars. Morality is applied through the power of moral memory, of the recall of virtuous actions and their connections, as a basis for the moral comprehension and guidance of a past action. Morality in this manner never becomes theoretical. It is always reason arising in human affairs as the exercise of prudence. Prudence engenders propriety, and propriety or decorum is the proper carrying out of one's station and its duties. Aristotle says, "Prudence is yoked to the virtue of one's character, and it is to prudence, if in fact the principles of prudence are in accord with the moral virtues and what is correct in the moral virtues accords with prudence."[93]

Pleasure is not separable from the virtues or from prudence. Pleasure is something whole and it is essential to the good life. Pleasure is not in itself happiness, but there is no happiness without pleasure: "without activity, pleasure does not arise, and pleasure completes every activity."[94] The one form of activity that guarantees pleasure is contemplation, because contemplation is self-sufficient. The use of the intellect for contemplation does not imply that we withdraw from society in order to contemplate, although it does require leisure. Contemplation is a way of life. Life is approached as something that can be reflected upon by the intellect even as we go about any of our affairs and actions.

Contemplation or *theōria*, *theōrein*, is, in its root meaning, to look upon or to observe (*thea*, action of seeing) and is that from which *theater* is derived and akin to *thauma* or wonder—the source of philosophy, according to Aristotle. Contemplation is the art of looking upon something in order to comprehend it and to do so for its own sake, without any pragmatic purpose. Contemplation is the activity that is most distinctive of a human being because it accords with the intellect: "This life, therefore, is also the happiest."[95] The excellence that is achieved by the use of the intellect produces a pleasure that can be sustained, but it does not replace pleasures that come and go in the body and passions. They have their place in the complete life. Neither does contemplation replace the role of the moral virtues that involve the body in its relation to the mind and the will. Moral excellence in this sense is required for contemplation to fulfill its role in the individual's life. But "if happiness is an activity in accord with virtue, it is reasonable that it would accord with the most excellent virtue, and this would be the virtue belonging to what is best."[96]

The result of contemplation or of looking upon the theater of the world is not the acquisition of knowledge for its own sake, for on the view I wish to hold, what is contemplated or seen in the theater of the world must be turned back upon the self in order that the self can pursue the knowledge of what it is to be a self. In the prominence of self-knowledge for the human being, the Socratic and the Aristotelian manners of moral philosophy must meet. This is the humanist ideal. The roles the human being plays are the means for the self-seeing necessary to the contemplative life. Contemplation, then,

93. Ibid., 1178a.
94. Ibid., 1175a.
95. Ibid., 1178a.
96. Ibid., 1177a.

is not itself a role but the ability to find and maintain continuity among all the human roles. Self-knowledge is the True that is grasped from seeing all of the human roles as a whole.

PART 2

The Labor of the Negative

INTRODUCTORY REMARKS

WHEN HEGEL's *PHENOMENOLOGY OF SPIRIT* appeared in 1807, the Republic of Letters, and specifically philosophical letters, came to possess for the first time a science of the experience of consciousness. This science offered a complete account, expressed in narrative form, of all the ways in which the world appears to the human self and which, when systematically comprehended, provide a resolution of the ancient quest for self-knowledge, originally announced as a moral precept on the walls of the pronaos of the Temple of Apollo at Delphi.

The reader of Hegel's work is taken in a dialectical progression of stages, from consciousness of the world as a mere succession of heres and nows, through all the forms of the human spirit, to the standpoint of absolute knowing, in which all of the stages can be recollected and internalized by consciousness, such that the True is grasped as the whole. But the journey that consciousness takes, from its most rudimentary form to its most self-conscious and self-determinate standpoint, is a highway of despair. The promise that each stage holds out, as consciousness first discovers it, soon turns into an illusion. Each particular stage, as it is fully entered and developed by consciousness, fails to provide consciousness with the means it seeks to grasp itself as a whole.

Consciousness slowly realizes that each way of grasping the world and itself as the knower of the object is defective. Each stage is a stage because it leaves something out and provides less than a way to grasp the totality of experience. Thus consciousness must at all points engage in the labor of the negative (*Arbeit des Negativen*). All truths are partial truths. On arriving at any truth, consciousness learns it must at the same time stare the negative in the face, for the negative—what is left out—has determinate content. What is not also has being and its being must be joined with what is or what appears to be. This realization leads consciousness to take a next step in its drive to comprehend experience as a whole.

Hegel's phenomenological principle of the negative, or "determinate negation," as he calls it, suggests a principle for the pursuit of moral philosophy. We must not only comprehend what constitutes the moral in its positive form and content, we must also attach this comprehension to a grasp of the form and content of the non-moral—the negative of the moral. The immoral is part of the moral and a part of moral inquiry, as expounded in Part 1. In the modern world, we prominently encounter the non-moral. The non-moral in this sense is the banal but dangerous form of the human condition.

These are forms of the human condition that do not arise from any true sense of the moral. They know nothing of the moral dimension of the human spirit, or are at best pseudo-moral. Yet they are forces to be reckoned with in the modern world, forces that can be confronted only by the practice of prudence. What follow are analyses of what I think to be the three most powerful non-moral embodiments of the human condition in our time. To an extent they have roots in earlier ages (especially the first two), but they come to the fore in our time, and unless we confront them as genuine negatives we will live in the illusion that the moral has a universal appeal to all human beings when, in fact, it does not. There are many among us who are without a moral nature. Upon the admission of this fact and a knowledge of the implications of this fact, moral philosophy depends.

2

Terrorism: The Ideology of Identity

TERRORISM AND THE HUMAN CONDITION

WE MAY EASILY SAY that terrorism can be found as a phenomenon throughout the ages of human society. In its general form, those in power and those who would seek power by revolutionary means have engaged in terrorism. It is a way to maintain as well as to seize power over others, and it is a common aspect of human warfare. In terms of the relations of individuals to one another, the terrorizing of one person by another, or even the use of terroristic threats, is against the law in most, if not all, human societies. Terrorism, in the classical sense, is limited in scope and effect and is often even local. But in the modern world, terrorism has assumed a particular form that trades upon or aspires to trade upon the phenomena of instant, electronic communication, air travel, and the international nature of modern economies and institutions. The modern terrorist is banal, not evil, an agent of ideology, not someone engaged in a moral act. What is the nature of modern terrorism? How can we confront it? How does it arise from the human condition itself?

Philosophical reflections on terrorism to date have focused on the political, historical, and cultural conditions of terrorism, its connections to the legacy of the Enlightenment, fundamentalism, and so forth.[1] They have not raised the fundamental question of who the terrorist is, how the being of

1. E.g., Borradori, *Philosophy in a Time of Terror*.

61

the terrorist arises from the conditions of human existence from which all types of lives are formed. This question is not merely theoretical. Its answer involves considerable practical, political, and ethical implications.

In order to consider the terrorist as a type of human being, we must be willing to entertain the proposition that terrorists are responsible for terrorism. This may seem an obvious claim. It may seem to be no more than a tautology. It is not. It is a claim about the cause of terrorism. Terrorists are not born but made, in the sense that all human beings make for themselves their own particular forms of selfhood by developing various patterns or types of lives as a response to the common conditions of human existence. Human animals are unique in this regard. They tacitly or consciously take the very fact of their existence as problematic and seek ways to realize their being as selves.

From this unique fact of human existence arises the ancient Greek question, what is the best life? The Greeks understood that the human world is divided into various fundamental types of lives, each being an answer to the nature of the human. As related in Part 1, Aristotle claims there is the life of the pursuit of pleasure, which is tied to the appetites; the life of politics, which pursues honor; and the life of contemplation, which is governed by the love of wisdom. In addition to these there is the pursuit of business or the life of money-making, which is more a means than an end.[2] In modern society these types of lives are expanded into an array of careers, which, taken together, are the basis of the cultural, political, and economic life of any nation. Two of these are directly responsible for the life of the state: the politician, through which the institution of government is maintained, and the warrior, through which the defense and security of the state is maintained.

In what way is the terrorist a part of this picture of the human condition—of man as a self-diversifying, social animal? The cultural and ethical relativist regards the terrorist as identical with the warrior, claiming that a terrorist is for one society what a warrior or "freedom fighter" is for another. My claim, in what follows, is that the terrorist is not a warrior or freedom fighter, that there is an absolute difference between the terrorist and the warrior. The intellectual confusion that typifies relativism prevents a clear comprehension of the nature of the terrorist and promotes the inability to distinguish the terrorist as a perverse human type from the warrior as a noble human type. Understanding terrorism in philosophical terms as a response by individuals to the human problems of self-identity and self-recognition in no sense preempts, nor should it preempt, other ways of understanding it: historically, socially, and psychologically. All ways of understanding

2. Aristotle, *Ethics* 1095b–96a.

terrorism and the terrorist should be pursued and coordinated in an effort to comprehend, and protect ourselves from, this form of violence.

My concern here is with what is generally thought of as international terrorism, as distinguished from domestic terrorism. I understand domestic terrorism to involve issues internal to a particular society in which terrorists, through violent and clandestine acts, attempt, in effect, to take law into their own hands. These acts of terrorism may be done by isolated individuals or groups, striking out against specific laws or policies of their own government, or they may be the result of separatist movements pursuing their cause. I regard international terrorism as organized acts of violence intended to dramatize a clash between opposing ways of life, to bring panic throughout a people or nation with the aim of causing it to suffer defeat of its economy and values, as though it had lost a war.

Those responsible for international acts of terrorism can be residents and citizens of the country in which their terrorist acts occur or they can be foreigners. When I use the words "terrorism" and "terrorist" I mean them in this international sense. I intend my analysis to be independent from any one example of terrorism, but I have come to my conclusions by meditating on radical, Islamic-inspired terrorism and its understanding of itself as being at war with Western democracy.

TERRORISM AND PRIMAL FEAR

Terror comes to English from Latin *terror*, from *terrere*, "to frighten," akin to the Greek *trein*, "to flee from fear." Terror is a state of intense fright, of stark fear. English, like Latin, makes a distinction between fear as an emotional state of the self marked by the feeling of danger or the expectation of danger, and terror. Terror can be the result of natural events such as earthquakes, hurricanes, or floods, as well as of human acts of violence. Terrorism is the systematic use of terror as a means of coercion, including the attempt to create an atmosphere of threat or violence, such as a reign of terror.

An act of terrorism is an attempt to incite the emotion of fear that is tied to the sense of self-preservation and heighten this fear to a level at which the recipient or recipients will feel victimized, unable to act freely and deliberately. The terrorist has the aim of making the terrorized lose the fundamental human sense of freedom, of self-determination. When this sense is lost, the natural power of human will is weakened. The selfhood of the terrorized is compromised such that the terrorism, if successful, destroys the confidence of the individual self in the larger selfhood of the society. The strength of a society depends upon its members having confidence in the commonweal. If terrorism is to be effective, the terrorist must affect the commonweal.

Among the passions of the soul, terror is the most primordial. Terror, as primordial, connects the human to the divine. Giambattista Vico, the eighteenth-century Italian philosopher of culture and history, connects terror with the first experience of the divine, from which originates the first social order, in his *New Science concerning the Common Nature of the Nations*. For Vico, the principles upon which humanity rests are religion, marriage, and burial.[3] Vico's primal scene is adopted from the biblical phenomenon of the universal flood, following which, for more than two centuries, the offspring of the sons of Noah become giants, *bestioni*, and roam the great forest of the earth.

Like Hobbes's first men, the *bestioni* are without human custom and their life is nasty, brutish, and short; but, unlike the Hobbesian first men, Vico's giants do not form society through a social covenant. Instead, they are humanized by the sudden appearance of lightning in the thunderous sky, caused by the drying out of the earth after the Flood. This new experience incites in the giants, who have wandered the earth without fear, the new feeling of terror (*spavento*). The giants shake in their great bodies with this unprecedented, all-encompassing fear, and they cry out. From this cry they speak the first word, "Jove," or *Jupiter Tonans*—Jove the Thunderer.

From this original moment of terror both religion and language are born. Their trembling and terror cause the first people to flee from the divine presence of the sky, into caves. There, males and females form marriages, from which come families, the rudiment of all social order. Those who found families establish lineages and property, which generates the distinctively human custom of burial, whereby ancestors are established. Vico's sense of the experience of the divine as full of extraordinary fear is similar to the conception of the holy (*das Heilige*) of Rudolph Otto, whose *Idea of the Holy* founds the history of religion. This conception of the sacred is borne out further by the work of Mircea Eliade, the twentieth-century historian of religion and mythologist.

The terrorist intends to be godlike, to break into the ordinary world of the terrorized as something from beyond. The act of the terrorist is not intended as the production of social order but as its inverse, the destruction of the social order of the terrorist's enemies. The intention of terrorist action is the reduction of social order to the original moment of chaos that marks the beginning of social order itself. The terrorist hopes that his enemies will lose the compass of their commonweal and approach a state of the war of

3. Vico, *New Science*, 97.

all against all—that is, a state of individuals all seeking their own ends in sustained panic, in conflict with each other and their former leaders. Terrorism, unlike war, is not the direct attempt to conquer an enemy. It is based on the belief that the enemy's society is internally weak, and that, once terrified, its citizens will allow their social bonds to collapse. Terrorists hold that they possess the superior values that will allow them to succeed once they master the most effective techniques of destruction.

THE WARRIOR AND TERRORIST AS HUMAN TYPES

Terrorists believe themselves to be warriors. Karl Jaspers, in *The Future of Mankind*, has characterized the warrior as a human type whose being is motivated by the conjunction of two principles: (1) the risk of one's life and (2) its risk for the sake of an ethical ideal.[4] The warrior is one of the ways within the human world that the problem of the meaning of life is confronted. The warrior is not a daredevil or adventurer; that is, the warrior's willingness to risk life is not based on motives of thrill or profit. Thrill and profit are products of desire—the desire for personal challenge, fame, or money—and, like appetites, thrill and profit are not virtues or ethical ideals.

The warrior is not a social reformer or a politician, not an agent for social change; the warrior neither reforms nor governs. The ethical ideal for which the warrior will risk life is not of the warrior's own making. This ideal is always the way of life of the warrior's society. The warrior need not simply in principle take up the ethical ideal from an established nation. As a human type, the figure of the warrior may be present in a revolution, rebellion, insurrection, or civil war aimed at bringing down an established political order. In so doing the revolutionary's aim is to make a new nation, to establish new ethical ideals by abandonment or a transformation of the old.

The art of the warrior is the art of war. The warrior is the human embodiment of just warfare. The warrior's commitment to the risk of life on behalf of an ethical ideal is absolute. It is parallel to the artist's absolute commitment to art, the believer's absolute commitment to religious reality, the thinker's absolute commitment to rational thought, and the citizen's absolute commitment to civility. All these commitments and similar ones are crucial to the order of the human world as distinctively human.

Why is the terrorist not a warrior representing the ethical ideal of a society opposed to one's own? The attempt to instill terror in the enemy is as old as warfare, ranging from the New Zealand Maori warriors' use of fierce facial expressions and masks to frighten the enemy (and inspire

4. Jaspers, *Future of Mankind*, chap. 4.

themselves), to the use of modern ordnance to produce "shock and awe." A terrified enemy is a weak enemy. Acts of sabotage behind enemy lines may not only destroy valuable facilities and materiel but may have the further benefit of instilling terror. Terror is part of human warfare, but the natural presence of terror in acts of warfare is not terrorism. Terrorism as a phenomenon of modern life is systematic violence directed against innocents in a population who are not enemies in a military sense, against which no recognized nation has declared war. Terrorism does not respect the laws of war—especially in that war is not deliberately made against innocents and civilians. Instead, terrorism is intended as a violation of this law. Terrorism makes no particular distinction between military and civilian targets in what it considers to be an enemy population. In fact, in its effort to cause panic, terrorism prefers civilian targets.

There are two kinds of terrorists, neither of which is a warrior. One kind of terrorist shares with the warrior the principle of risk of life but hopes not to die. This terrorist aspires to commit an act of terrorism and escape. The other kind of terrorist intends to lose his or her life in a violent act of suicide-homicide. This kind of terrorist inverts the first principle of the warrior. Both kinds of terrorists appear to share with the warrior the second principle of the warrior's existence—action on behalf of an ethical ideal— but they do not. To claim to be acting in accordance with an ethical ideal does not mean one is actually so doing. An ethical ideal is different from an ideology. The warrior does not invent or devise the ethical ideal guiding his or her risk of life. The warrior receives this ideal from the authority of the nation on behalf of which the warrior acts. The warrior is upholding and defending the nation's way of life, its ideals as they have been realized in its customs, laws, traditions, history, and everyday life. The warrior upholds and defends what the nation is as a whole. The warrior as revolutionary upholds the ethical ideal of what the new nation will be.

The terrorist is a self-appointed soldier acting on behalf of a personal, political, or religious ideology. An ideology is not a morality; it only seems to be such in that it is intended to provide justification for the believer's actions. In the sense that courage, as a virtue, is different from determination or willpower, an ethical ideal is different from an ideology. An ethical ideal, a virtue that guides actions, is supra-individual; it is more than what can be attained in the actions that are guided by it. In contrast, an ideology makes its aims and values completely attainable. It is formulated by the individual or group completely in their own terms, a perfect reflection of their own temperament and grasp of the world. It is dogmatic. Ideologies are not made from thin air. They are selective formulations taken from existing political, social, and religious traditions. Because they are built through such selections, ideologies seem to be ideals brought forth from genuine human moral sensibility. The terrorist does not know the difference between an ethical ideal and an ideology and mistakes one for the other. An ideology is inherently perverse because it inverts the power of moral sense that is the distinctive feature of human consciousness.

An ideology seems invincible because it cannot be modified. The suicide bomber is the perfect human counterpoint to the apparent invincibility of the ideology because his or her actions, if not thwarted by incompetence or discovery, are absolute. The sense of absoluteness that attends both ideology and suicide is appealing to the mentality of the suicide bomber. All-important for a suicide bomber is the belief that he or she can attain glory by dying for the certainties portrayed in the ideology. This desire for glorification can produce self-recruitment of suicide bombers, who may form cells and assume an ideology taken from what is expressed by clerics or terrorist figures.

Suicide bombers may also be recruited by leaders and managers, who do not tie bombs to themselves. Such suicide bombers function in a manner analogous to the "mules" recruited by drug cartels to carry drugs across international borders. The drug mules are motivated by greed, the suicide bombers by a need for glory and seeming completion of a fragmented self, accomplished in a single act.

These clerics or terrorist figures may see themselves as moral leaders or fundamentalist revolutionaries, but they are not. They are driven by their own arrogance and need for reputation. Osama bin Laden was not a revolutionary; he was a celebrity, taken with his own will to power. He was not an astute political analyst or military strategist. He had little real knowledge of his adversary, the West, and no significant personal experience of it. The same can be said of the radical Muslim clerics both within and without Islamic countries who advocate destruction of Western democracy. In no Western nation are Muslims prevented in any significant sense from practicing their faith, yet the theme of such clerics is the oppression of their faith.

It is not possible to negotiate with Islamic terrorists because their cause is cosmic. It is not political. It is metaphysical—the defeat and destruction of the other, the infidel, the West. There is no nation or specific political organization that Islamic terrorists represent. There is no entity with which to negotiate. The terrorized find themselves in the position of attempting to speculate on what the demands of the terrorists might be and what may be the causes of their actions. But the terrorists have an indefinite number of demands and causes—claiming whatever seems most plausible at the moment. A commonly expressed view has been that the war in Iraq was responsible for Islamic terrorism against the West. Such a view forgot that the African embassy bombings, the attack on the World Trade Center and Pentagon of September 11, 2001, and the earlier vehicle bombing of the World Trade Center occurred before this war. This view also forgot the attack on the Navy destroyer USS *Cole* on October 12, 2000, while it refueled in the Yemeni port of Aden, for which al-Qaeda claimed responsibility.

The cosmic or nonpolitical nature of this kind of terrorism can be seen in its difference from the use of terrorism by national separatist movements. Such movements are political; they have specific goals and identifiable orders of organization; they employ terrorism as a tactic. The violence of their acts is typically self-limited, intended not to kill a great number of people but to show their presence and their power. The intent of international, Islamic terrorism is to institute havoc, to kill and maim as many people as possible. Their mission is without limit; they have no real political demands, and the cause of their actions is the inherent evil of the other. The real cause of Islamic terrorism is this mindset.

A unique example of modern terrorism is the kamikaze pilots of the Japanese Air Force of World War II. This form of terrorism was military terrorism, not directed against civilian populations. The kamikaze pilots who flew suicide missions into U.S. ships at sea were warriors who abandoned the warrior's principle of self-survival for the glory of their emperor and their country. As a method of warfare, the kamikaze program was a failure. It did not destroy the U.S. fleet nor win the war.

In this fact is a great truth about terrorism. There is no evidence that terrorist acts—no matter how cosmic in conception or how well executed—have any ability to bring down the order of an established society or its military power. Despite all the suicide bombings directed by Hamas, Hezbollah ("Party of God"), and other, smaller terrorist groups, Israel still stands. Despite al-Qaeda's attack of 9/11, the United States, its economy, political system, and military are intact. Despite the terrorist bombings of the London transit system in the summer of 2005 and the thwarted attempt to blow up flights from the United Kingdom to the United States during the summer of 2006, British society still stands and functions. War, revolution, and rebellion bring down societies and governments. Terrorism does not. There is no evidence that terrorists can more than momentarily affect a people's evolved way of life. The 2004 terrorist train bombing in Madrid may have affected its national election and immediate policies, but it has effected no fundamental change in Spain as a democratic society. Despite the suicide bombings of the Red Sea resort of Sharm el-Sheik in late July 2005, which killed foreign tourists as well as many Egyptian citizens, the country and culture of Egypt remain.

For the terrorist, terrorism can become an end in itself. The November 2005 hotel bombings in Aman, Jordan, that killed fifty-seven innocent people and injured many others is an example of this phenomenon. To blow oneself up in the middle of a Muslim wedding party attended by ordinary families—adults and children—as was the case in the Radisson SAS Hotel, has no imaginable purpose in real politics. Such acts have lost all direction and are comprehensible only as crimes against humanity. The immediate outrage and demonstrations of the Jordanian people were evidence of this, and these bombings were counterproductive for al-Qaeda's image in the Arab world.

Such bombings have an analogy with the actions of urban revolutionaries in the United States who several decades ago robbed banks to finance their cause (e.g., the so-called Symbionese Liberation Army). After meeting with some success in robbing banks, the "revolutionaries" became just bank robbers, common criminals caught up in the process itself, without any clear sense of purpose.

Terrorism in modern technological society, as opposed to traditional society, depends greatly on the media and on the totality of modern society, the interconnection of all its functions. In earlier forms of human society a terrorist act remained local, affecting only a limited number of people. News of a terrorist act traveled slowly in such societies and could have little broad effect. In modern society any terrorist act reverberates immediately around the world. The interconnectedness of all orders and activities of life brought about by the linking of techniques of production, social management, communication, and information allows what affects one sector of a society to reverberate through the society as a whole and to go beyond its borders.

Much confusion can surround who the terrorist really is because he or she is not a simple opposite of the warrior. The terrorist, for example, is not a criminal, and it is a mistake to treat the terrorist as such, to attribute to him or her, if captured, the right of a criminal prosecution. A criminal breaks laws for his or her own gain or because of psychological motivations. No one need mistake a criminal for a warrior. The terrorist as a human type is dangerous because he or she is so close to the truth of the warrior's existence. He or she can appear, to those who are unable to think clearly, to be a warrior attached to a different doctrine. Thus discussion about the terrorist falls into the paralogisms of relativism.

The terrorist perhaps seems to have, like the warrior, the virtues of courage and honor—the courage of his or her convictions, not ours, his or her sense of honor, not ours—and thus seems to be capable of heroism. Grand illusions are grand because they are so close to the truth. The most

69

dangerous illusion is one that is not simply a partial truth but one that is nearly indistinguishable from the true and the real. Arrogance is not courage, nor is it honor, although it may be mistaken for such, especially by the arrogant. The bad faith of the terrorist is to believe himself or herself to be a warrior. It is a state that is always self-reifying because the terrorist never considers the possibility that the ills he or she seeks revenge against are not of the other's making. The terrorist's answer to "What went wrong?" is always that the other has caused it.

An account of this point, written and in press just prior to the events of 9/11, is Bernard Lewis, *What Went Wrong*, which is developed further in his *Crisis in Islam*. Lewis shows how the separation of the religious and the secular has allowed the West, from the early modern period, to develop conceptions of individualism, law, social institutions, and scientific thinking. The Islamic world, which in earlier periods of history had surpassed the West in intellectual achievements, has been left behind, due to the inability to separate church and state and to respond to these developments of the West in a positive way.

TERRORISM AS CARGO CULT

If terrorism is ultimately useless as a military or political device, why does it persist? One explanation may be that terrorists and their leaders and believers are essentially migrants of identity, a version of a cargo-cult mentality. "Cargo cult" is an anthropological term derived from the behavior of tribes inhabiting remote regions in the South Pacific, especially Papua New Guinea and the Melanesian Islands. The phenomenon has roots in the mid-1800s but most recently refers to the reaction of native inhabitants to goods delivered to these islands as military cargo by airplanes and ships during World War II. The inhabitants witnessed an array of goods they could themselves never produce and regarded these wonders as a gift the gods had given to those who possessed them.

"Cargo cult" specifically designates the phenomenon of an indigenous population, colonized by a developed nation, believing that it could acquire all the goods and advantages owned by the colonizers, through messianic dedication to a divine power that would at some crucial point bestow all such blessings on them, making them equal or superior to their colonizers. As with all cult behavior, this often meant assembling with the cult leaders at a particular date or place to await a world-changing event. For many cargo-cult movements this meant a return of their ancestors in ships or planes, delivering goods that would meet all their needs and make work unnecessary.

There are striking parallels between the current Islamic terrorist cults and the Pacific cargo cults. What the Islamic cults add is systematic violence. The classic cargo cults are based on a belief that what is desired will come about through a break in being. Through a proper alignment between the human order and the divine, the human order will be perfected in a single moment. The human order will receive what it deserves and desires, as a gift of the divine order. All will be put right because of human fidelity. The material goods and social benefits the colonized desire are not sought by political ingenuity, hard work, and pragmatism. There is no notion that the solution to the under position of the colonized is to negotiate, advance, organize, and gain the ability to produce what the colonizers have learned to produce. Nor is there a will toward the organization of an army of liberation and the enactment of revolution or civil war. The solution is envisioned not in political but in metaphysical terms.

The program of terrorism of the Islamic cults is very similar. Jihad, the principle of a holy war, is moved from the idea of war to the idea of terrorism, as if terrorism is a genuine form of warfare. To organize and raise an army to engage in real war is a difficult process. Terrorism requires much less. What is hoped in the terrorist act or series of acts is that, with the help of Allah, the societies of the infidel oppressor will fall. Since there is no principle of practical politics or military science that would claim terrorism to be an effective device, the justification for terrorism is metaphysical, theological, and religious. The power that the West possesses will fall through acts of divinely inspired violence. The West has no true relation to the divine and so it is ultimately defenseless. This internal weakness and lack of fortitude is the analysis of the West found in the writing of Sayyid Qutb.[5] A genuine way to confront the unsatisfactory conditions—the lack of the ability to produce from within their own resources and will the fruits of technological society that the West enjoys by means of imitating and learning new skills and new secular forms of political order—is not considered. Social pragmatism is not an option to be taken. The terrorist never has a politically positive program.

The cause of all difficulties in Islamic society, according to the Islamic cults, is the arrogance of power of the West. It is arrogance as well as spiritual weakness that they attribute to their declared enemy. But the fundamental flaw of the Islamic cults is their own arrogance. They have no principle of self-evaluation. Politics works through power. Terrorism seems to be power, but it is not real power; although terrorist acts are sensational,

---

5. Berman, "Philosopher of Islamic Terror."

they are ineffective. Until terrorists realize this they will remain as puzzled about their real lack of success as were the cargo cultists, gathered on the hill at the appropriate time with their leaders to receive the gift that was not to be given.

THE TERRORIST'S ARROGANCE AND THE LACK OF INNER WORTH

If terrorists are not warriors, what are they? The ever-present claim is that they are martyrs. No person committing suicide is a martyr. A martyr gives up his or her life for what is ethical and holy. But a martyr meets death at the hands of others, and the martyr's death is to teach a moral and religious lesson. The martyr dies for innocence. The martyr makes no one—not even enemies—the worse for his or her deeds or presence in the world. The martyr is the opposite human type to the terrorist. Once again the terrorist's being is realized as inversion.

We might say the terrorist is an agent of revenge, acting on behalf of a wronged and oppressed people. Revenge is not a virtue. There is no Aristotelian mean for which revenge is the middle of two extremes. Revenge is not a right under any rational system of law. There is no right of revenge. Revenge is the inverse of the virtue of justice, upon which all true social order is founded. Revenge may be a natural appetite, a reaction to a wrong or perceived wrong, but it is the opposite of virtue and reason.

To invert is to turn something upside down from what it is in its proper state. The terrorist, seen from every perspective, is the inverse of the proper or positive determination of the human condition. The terrorist is not a warrior seen from one perspective and a terrorist from another. Seen from the perspective of the human being itself, the terrorist is the inversion of moral excellence.

In the end, the terrorist's death is meaningless. That is why there is so much effort expended to attempt to glorify it. It is meaningless because in practical terms terrorism fails to accomplish its end and because no virtue adheres to the being of the terrorist. The terrorist as a human type has no inherent value. Of the four cardinal virtues, no wisdom, justice, or moderation adheres to the terrorist's formulation of the human. Does the virtue of courage in some way apply to the terrorist? As mentioned above, one might claim that, even though inverted, the terrorist at least exemplifies courage. Courage is the virtue that produces honor. Courage is the virtue of the hero and of the warrior, who is always capable of heroic action. Certainly it takes determination, mustered at some point, to carry out the act of a suicide bombing. But is it admirable? Is it admirable to kill the innocent? Is it admirable to kill oneself? Courage is a virtue tied to risk and the attempt to overcome a danger—for the self, through its action, to go beyond the self. An act of courage allows the agent to transcend conditions and, if possible, to prevail.

For an act to be courageous, the ethical ideal that motivates it must be valid. The terrorist's aim of killing innocents has no validity. No meaning for human existence can come from it. In the end, it is a hollow act. To kill innocents in the manner of the international terrorist is to commit a crime against humanity. Such an act is not courageous because it is not admirable. The individual terrorist may require courage in the psychological sense of willpower, but courage in its ethical sense cannot be attached to the terrorist's actions.

The arrogance of the terrorist, what he or she mistakes for courage and honor, prevents the terrorist from being a just soul. Arrogance prevents the terrorist from any attraction to *sōphrosynē*—that power of self-control, temperance, or moderation that produces moral sanity, or *harmonia*, among the appetites and spirit and the rational parts of the soul and that can function as the mean between the extremes of pleasure and pain. Without access to *sōphrosynē* the terrorist has no access to the formation of a just soul. The failure of soul induced by arrogance makes impossible the proportion among the parts of the soul that is the key to their internal harmony. Revenge appears to the terrorist to be justice. Revenge accomplished by the attack on the other, who is seen as the cause of the injustice claimed by the terrorist, appears as the means to justice. Justice is thus understood as external to the self rather than as the essence of the self.

The terrorist's arrogance makes freedom a matter of external conditions. For the terrorist, freedom has been taken away by the other, as the other is the cause of what went wrong. For the terrorist, to reduce the other to a state of intense fear is to produce freedom. Freedom is seen as the power to dominate. Terrorism is a fantasy of freedom acted out. It is a fantasy because terrorist acts, in terms of real politics, as said above, never have the power to bring down governments. They do so only in the minds of terrorists. The source of the Islamic terrorist's fantasy is religion. The terrorist sees the world in terms of the mythico-religious division of the world into the sacred and the profane, the believer and the infidel, the light and the darkness. The battle with the other is a battle of light and darkness, with the terrorist as the agent of God's will. It is an ancient struggle that stands against a rational conception of freedom.

Freedom, like justice, is the power of self-determination, as discussed in Part 1. Arrogance appears to be self-determination; thus it is such a dangerous illusion. The terrorist appears to be the most self-determined of all, yet his terrorism has no positive content. The terrorist's actions are only part of a pre-ethical, mythico-religious drama of opposites. Freedom as self-determination is a process whereby an individual or group or society draws upon the resources available to it to develop its own reality, to set its own purposes and ends.

Through arrogance the terrorist is also cut off from dignity. Human dignity accompanies human freedom in the process of self-determination. Neither self-destruction nor the risk of life for revenge has any dignity. The terrorist always takes himself or herself seriously, and in this seriousness the terrorist believes he or she commands dignity, but this illusion of self-worth depends on the confrontation with the other. Respect is dependent on the fear that the other is supposed to show, making the terrorist feel all-powerful. This sense of respect is external and is not based on self-respect. Dignity or inner worth, when developed in the self of the individual, makes the individual a presence in the world. This is a course cut off from the condition of the terrorist, whose self-worth is tied to his or her role in the battle with the other—with the nonbeliever, the darkness, the evil, the cause of all that has gone wrong.

Our task is to comprehend the terrorist as a human type, not in order to reform, to offer therapy, or to cure but to eliminate him or her when found. The greatest obstacle to combating terrorism is the view that the terrorist is a victim. This conception of the victim is part of the ideology of cultural relativism that is at the heart of political correctness. In accord with the victim mentality of cultural relativism, we, the terrorist's other, are to believe that the conditions of the terrorist's life have become so bad and that he or she feels so humiliated as to be driven to terrorism.

In this way the victim or potential victim of the terrorist sees the terrorist as a victim, a victim of the success of the Western, democratic, technological society that the terrorist takes as other. The cultural relativist feels guilty for his or her good fortune. Thus the cultural relativist believes that the terrorist must be understood and helped—that there must be a reason for the terrorist's acting as he or she does, that the terrorist must somehow have suffered at our hands, that he or she is not responsible for the terrorist acts committed but that we, as the other, are responsible. The success of Western society, of its way of life, is then equated with arrogance and dominance of the less fortunate. Such self-deprecation makes us believe that it is the terrorist who is the victim, rather than we whom he or she wishes to kill—and will kill, if given the opportunity. This view of ourselves, not the terrorist, as arrogant is a failure of our own self-respect. This failure of self-respect leads to the idea of reconciliation.

The idea of reconciliation is the most dangerous idea of all, for there is no reconciliation with the terrorist as a form of selfhood, a human type. With the idea that the terrorist is somehow a victim we reach the most dangerous point of the contemporary phenomenon of terrorism. Only if such mentality of reconciliation or pacification or charity toward the terrorist can be overcome can we save ourselves. For any anti-terrorist program to be used effectively, this mentality of reconciliation must be overcome. It can be overcome only by a precise recognition of the nature of the terrorist.

Terrorists are the cause of terrorism. The terrorized are not the cause; they do not bring terrorism on themselves. The view that if the subjects of terror were not who they are, or if their governments acted differently toward those countries from which the terrorists emerge, then the terrorists would not act as they do, is false. The terrorist's logic of the cargo cult constructs the world in a very ancient way and involves the return to the categories of pre-ethical or mythical thought, such that the mind of the modern terrorist divides the world into sacred and profane, into the faithful and the infidel. All acts are justified that can be done in the name of the sacred. Action is referred for its justification to what is accessible in ideological terms. Once this ideology, made from this pre-ethical sense of the sacred, becomes the standard for human conduct, the fanatical and fantastic realm of the terrorist is possible.

My aim in these remarks has been to show that it is possible epistemologically and ethically to comprehend who the terrorist is. My aim is a call for prudence. There is a tendency to intellectualize terrorism away, to turn it into an issue of political and historical argument. This response is a form of denial, a failure to admit straightaway the danger of the new phenomenon of international terrorism and the need truly to comprehend it in order prudently to confront it.

Prudence, as discussed in Part 1 in relation to the virtues, is a labor of the positive, an application of correct reason to guide choice, develop moral character, and aim at the good and at happiness. Prudence, here and in relation to the phenomenon of psycho-sociopathy in the following chapter, is of a different kind. It is the application of correct reason as a labor of the negative, for in this regard to be prudent is to aim at self-protection from the threat of non-moral acts or agents. Only if prudence can be practiced in this sense, as a way to confront the negative, can we be at liberty to engage in prudence in the classic sense of pursuing virtue.

In the world of action, not thought, the task of protecting the innocent falls to the opposite of the terrorist—the warrior. The warrior is the human type upon whom those subjected to terror must immediately depend, both in the sense of the warrior as a specialized profession and in the sense of the temperament of the warrior that is inherent in the true citizen of the nation. The response to the terrorist by both the warrior and the citizen must be clearheaded and uncompromising.

There is no response to terrorism that can be achieved by ethical discourse. The terrorist stands outside humanity and thus outside any principle of morality, whether it be based on rational imperative, utility, or any other ethical position. The young Nigerian Umar Farouk Abdulmutallab, the "underwear bomber"—so called because of the explosives concealed in his underwear—who failed in his attempt to blow up an international flight as it was arriving in Detroit on Christmas Day in 2009, declared at his sentencing three years later, "I am glad to kill in the name of God."

The standpoint of the terrorist, in objective terms, is a false claim to morality. Morality is replaced by ideology that pretends to be a moral position but that is non-moral. Revenge is outside the discourse of vices and virtues. The quest for revenge of ills real or imagined can only be met by prudence. Prudence requires an accurate comprehension of the state of affairs in question and the willingness to act in accord with self-protection. Such response, if not simply expedient but truly prudent, requires us to meet terrorism with force, but not violence. Force must be guided by the cardinal virtues of courage, wisdom, moderation, and justice.

How the terrorist and terrorism are to be confronted in any particular situation or instance cannot be determined in advance. There is no general method that can be applied beyond the tactics practiced by law enforcement and the military. But these tactics, when properly guided by prudence, are all we have to prevent and meet the menace of the terrorist.

3

Psycho-Sociopathy:
The Counterfeit of Conscience

MORAL UNIVERSALITY

THE PSYCHO-SOCIOPATH IS ANOTHER type of threat to the peace and security of the lives of ordinary citizens for which moral philosophy must account. The threat of the terrorist is not a subtle threat. The terrorist may live among us unnoticed until his or her overt act of terrorism is performed. But the fact of terrorism, whether arising internally or externally, is well known. Its threat is a part of modern life. The threat of the psycho-sociopath is a subtle threat. We live constantly among persons with psycho-sociopathic personalities, and they do harm, often without our realizing that they are the cause of disruption in our individual lives. They are not planning our destruction, but their actions are not in any way governed by conscience or moral concerns. In their strategic pursuit of personal power and self-interest, they can affect and even ruin individual lives on a one-to-one basis.

Moral philosophy in all its contemporary forms, whether consequentialist, formalist, contractarian, utilitarian, or virtue ethicist, presumes the possibility of formulating principles of conduct that apply universally to all human beings. Standard exceptions are infants and young children, persons who are clinically insane, and persons with reduced mental capacity. These exceptions are recognized by all modern systems of morality and law. The inability to distinguish right from wrong, due to immature age, mental disorganization, or insufficient intelligence, is grounds to exempt any given person from moral responsibility and moral agency.

Human beings not bound by such conditions are distinguished by their capacity to have a moral response to the world and to be able to act, reflect, and reason in accord with this response. The human family depends upon the existence and actuality of this moral sensibility to motivate care for the young, the impaired, the ill, and the insane, as well as to maintain the ordinary connections and obligations among persons that make human society possible. Fundamental moral principles found in religions, moral philosophies, social customs, and systems of laws reflect the results of the activity caused by this moral sense of things. Moral sense is the interior of the ordinary human being, the basis of our freedom and self-determination.

Applied ethics as it has developed over the past several decades has given much attention to arguments concerning the status, treatment, and general care of those persons in the various aspects of the human condition I have mentioned, but it has not applied its ethical reasoning to the problem of the psycho-sociopath. The problem posed by the psycho-sociopath in human society is not a problem that has been forgotten in contemporary ethics; it is a problem that has not even been realized by the ethicist, whether pursuing problems in applied ethics or in ethical theory. A reason for this neglect is the conception of ethics as based in logical analysis apart from any connection with the senses of communication and conduct found in rhetoric.

Arguments in applied ethics, as stated in Part 1, are largely conducted in a purely pro-and-con fashion without any attention to the broader senses of language and moral narratives of which they are a part. This broader sense of things requires what can be called rhetorical philosophy. This rhetorical sense of philosophy goes beyond the simple exchange of arguments and can be closely allied to moral philosophy. I wish to suggest that the unique problem the psycho-sociopath poses for ethical life requires the perspective that can be obtained only by casting moral philosophy in rhetorical terms. I will return to this connection after characterizing the problem the psycho-sociopath presents to ethical thought. It is a unique problem that requires a unique perspective.

Analysis of the psycho-sociopath as a pernicious human type in the fields of psychiatry and psychotherapy is little more than sixty years old. Today it remains a pathological condition without a therapeutic solution and a problem with which few psychiatrists and psychotherapists wish to deal. It is an open question whether sociopathy is a mental illness, as there is no known cure or course of therapy. The psycho-sociopath is an aberrant personality, but it has no clear parallels with other mental disease.

What does the existence of the psycho-sociopath as a part of human society signify for moral philosophy? What can moral philosophy contribute to our understanding of the psycho-sociopath? For many readers the psycho-sociopath may be a phenomenon of which they have heard only in crime reports and television programs.[1] A basis for the philosophical, rhetorical, and moral grasp of the nature of the psycho-sociopath can be found in Plato's tale of the ring of Gyges. It at least offers a starting point where none at present exists.

THE RING OF GYGES

The ring of Gyges poses the problem that lies at the center of Western ethics: the difference between the just and the unjust life and whether there are grounds on which to choose the just over the unjust. In the first book of Plato's *Republic* the great sophist Thrasymachus introduces his view of justice (*dikaiosynē*) by attempting to insult Socrates. He asks Socrates if he has a wet nurse, because he needs someone to wipe his nose and to see to his basic education. He says Socrates does not "even know about sheep and shepherds."[2] He claims Socrates believes that shepherds are concerned with the welfare of their flocks as such and does not understand that shepherds fatten and care for their sheep simply for their own and their master's advantage. Because Socrates does not understand the nature of the shepherd's relation to the sheep, Thrasymachus says to him, "You believe that rulers in cities—true rulers, that is—think about their subjects differently than one does about sheep, and that night and day they think of something besides their own advantage. You are so far from understanding about justice and what's just, about injustice and what's unjust, that you don't realize that justice is really the good of another, the advantage of the stronger and the ruler, and harmful to the one who obeys and serves."[3]

Justice, then, is determined by convention, and the standard of convention is set by the stronger and the interest of the stronger. What is more, Thrasymachus holds, injustice dominates those who are just and who make themselves unhappy by their service to those who rule them and gain from

---

1. For an overview, see Seabrook, "Suffering Souls"; Burroughs, *Wolf at the Table*; and Gann, "Chameleon."

2. Plato, *Republic* 343a.

3. Ibid. 343b–c.

them. Thrasymachus says, "A just man always gets less than an unjust one."[4] The conventional good citizen who abides by propriety and the laws gets less and is deluded by a kind of morality that perceives the ruler to be acting in the interest of the ruled. The ruler follows propriety and the laws only to the extent they are advantageous. The shepherd fattens the sheep but never puts their welfare before his own.

In the second book of the *Republic*, Plato reintroduces the shepherd and the opposition between justice and injustice, not in terms of the ruler and the ruled but in terms of individual choice. The ring of Gyges is introduced by an argument that laws are the result of a social contract based on the fact that to do injustice is naturally good but to suffer injustice is naturally bad. The laws define what is just, and justice is only the intermediate between these extremes. People value justice "not as a good but because they are too weak to do injustice with impunity."[5] We are just and follow the laws because of faintness of heart. If we were free of any concern of being apprehended and suffering penalty, then we would do whatever we wish.

To visualize this possibility, Plato recalls the tale of the power that he says was possessed by "the ancestor of Gyges of Lydia" who was "a shepherd in the service of the ruler of Lydia."[6] While he was tending his sheep, a thunderstorm and an earthquake occurred, creating a chasm in the earth. The shepherd entered the chasm and discovered a hollow bronze horse, inside of which was a corpse, naked but for a gold ring on its finger. He took the ring and left the chasm. In a meeting at which he regularly reported the state of the flocks, the shepherd happened to turn the setting of the ring to the inside of his hand, whereupon he realized that he had immediately become invisible. The others proceeded with no awareness of his presence. When he turned the ring back, he became visible again. Having become aware of his new power, he arranged to become one of the group's messengers to report to the king. When he arrived he seduced the king's wife, and with her help killed the king and assumed the rule of the kingdom.

Plato writes, "Let's suppose, then, that there were two such rings, one worn by a just and the other by an unjust person. Now, no one, it seems, would be so incorruptible that he would stay on the path of justice or stay away from other people's property, when he could take whatever he wanted from the marketplace with impunity, go into people's houses and have sex with anyone he wished, kill or release from prison anyone he wished, and do

---

4. Ibid. 343d.
5. Ibid. 359a–b.
6. Ibid. 359c–d. Cf. Herodotus, *Persian Wars* 1.8.15.

all the other things that would make him like a god among humans."[7] Over and against this portrait of the unjust person, Plato says, we must consider the noble and just person, such as Amphiaraus in Aeschylus's *Seven Against Thebes*, who "did not wish to be believed to be the best but to be it."[8] The remainder of the *Republic* is the answer to the challenge begun by Thrasymachus and reformulated in the tale of the ring of Gyges.

In the tenth book of the *Republic*, just prior to Socrates' telling the myth of Er, in which the souls must choose the type of life into which they will be reincarnated, Socrates returns to the tale of Gyges: "And haven't we cleared away the various other objections to our argument without having to invoke the rewards and reputations of justice, as you said Homer and Hesiod did? And haven't we found that justice itself is the best thing for the soul [*psychē*] itself, and that the soul—whether it has the ring of Gyges or even it together with the cap of Hades—should do just things?"[9] The cap of Hades was likewise said to make its wearer invisible.

The tale of the ring of Gyges captures the being of the psycho-sociopath. The psycho-sociopathic personality knows, without question, that it possesses the ring of Gyges and the cap of Hades. No Platonic argument concerning the nobility and necessity of the just life can change the psycho-sociopath because he accepts without question the fact that he is invisible. The sociopath can masquerade as an ordinary person, passing through the world of such persons, being able to manipulate them to attain his own ends and, by outsmarting them, avoiding any adverse consequences or penalties. He is invisible due to his command of the purely sophistic art of rhetoric, the art that Thrasymachus teaches. (Although there are both male and female sociopaths, I will follow the convention of the clinical literature and employ the masculine pronoun throughout my discussion.) The psycho-sociopath is the master of the lie, the deceit, the dissimulation. The psycho-sociopath is bereft of all interior life. He has no emotions, which are the seat of moral sensibility and obligation. Like the ancestor of Gyges, he has no basis in his personality to cause him to seek a principle of order in his psyche that typifies the Platonic virtue of justice.

We might here join to Plato's consideration of the difference between justice and injustice Spinoza's analysis of the emotions. The way leading to freedom, for Spinoza, depends upon the cultivation of reason in order to control the emotions or affects (*affectiones*). Spinoza writes, at the beginning

7. Plato, *Republic* 360b–c.

8. Ibid.

9. Ibid. 612a–b. On the cap of Hades, see Homer, *Iliad* 8.44; cf. Aristophanes, *Acharnians* 390.

of the fourth part of the *Ethics*, "of human bondage": "Human infirmity in moderating and checking the emotions I name bondage: for, when a man is a prey to his emotions, he is not his own master, but lies at the mercy of fortune: so much so, that he is often compelled, while seeing that which is better for him, to follow that which is worse."[10]

The psycho-sociopath is absolutely without emotions and so is from the start free of their bondage. He is free of all guilt that arises from our grasp of the difference between good and evil. He is always potentially the stronger in any human relationship because he can pursue it without any need to master his feelings. The psycho-sociopath has no feelings. He passes invisibly through the human world because he impersonates the human person in the way the unjust man impersonates the just in order to gain his interests and power. The psychology of the human that underlies both Platonic and Spinozistic ethics (although they are different ethics) is the relationship between reason and emotions that produces moral sensibility.

Without this relationship within the psyche there are no moral problems for the human person. Completely free of any emotional reaction to others or to the world, the psycho-sociopath may pursue his own ends as freely as one who wears the ring of Gyges or cap of Hades. As he passes through the human world he need only keep his wits about him in order not to make mistakes and suffer consequences. He knows himself to be superior to others who are governed and handicapped by a sense of virtue and justice. He regards the emotional and moral motivations of others as weakness, making those others vulnerable to his power. He sees himself as a god among humans.

What the ring of Gyges in classical moral philosophy can only hypothesize is actualized in the psycho-sociopath, as uncovered by modern psychiatry and psychotherapy. What is the full profile of the psycho-sociopath as it is put forward by those concerned with researching it in these fields and with communicating its nature to the public? And where may we find principles of conduct that will allow us to deal with the psycho-sociopath in our midst?

THE PSYCHO-SOCIOPATH

It is not possible in a few pages to provide a complete picture of the psycho-sociopathic personality. The existence of such persons was clinically recognized in the early nineteenth century. The disorder was called "moral

10. Spinoza, *Ethics*, in *Chief Works*, 187.

insanity," which remains one of its clearest designations.[11] By the turn of the century and throughout the first half of the twentieth century it was termed "psychopathic personality" and later "antisocial personality disorder." These designations persist, together with the term *sociopath*. Clinically there seems to be no precise separation in the use of these modern terms. Because of the variations of what to call the type of personality in question I have generally used the term *psycho-sociopath*.

There seems to be a distinction between two types of psycho-sociopaths, but both types have no conscience or moral sense. For some their pathology leads them to become criminals or to engage in overt antisocial behavior or lifestyle. For others their pathology remains largely invisible, allowing them to treat others always as means and through this power to become successful in business and the professions, never suffering from any inhibitions as to how they achieve their ends. This type is antisocial in the more subtle sense of never being able to form friendships, relationships, and associations typical of persons with emotional lives and moral sensibilities, although the psycho-sociopath learns quickly to simulate these bonds and the emotions that accompany them, in order to manipulate others.

My comments in this section are based on three classic works in the field, the titles of which are instructive. They are written by clinicians with extensive experience and knowledge of the technical literature whose purpose is to explain what is known of the nature of the psycho-sociopath to the public. The classic work on this disorder is Hervey Cleckley, *The Mask of Sanity*, first published in 1941 and now in its fifth edition, printed in 1988 (Cleckley died in 1984). Robert D. Hare, *Without Conscience: The Disturbing World of the Psychopaths Among Us* (1993), contains a summary of the author's Psychopathy Checklist, which has become a diagnostic and research instrument in the study of the disorder.[12] Using the principles for diagnosing "antisocial personality disorder" in the fourth edition of the *Diagnostic and Statistical Manual of Mental Disorders* of the American Psychiatric Association, as well as sources in the literature, Martha Stout, in *The Sociopath Next Door* (2005), makes the striking claim that 4 percent of the population is sociopathic, or about one in twenty-five persons in the United States.[13]

Stout, comparing this rate to that of other diseases and disorders, writes, "there are more sociopaths among us than people who suffer from the much-publicized disorder of anorexia, four times as many sociopaths as schizophrenics, and one hundred times as many sociopaths as people

11. Cleckley, *Mask*, 226.
12. Hare, *Conscience*, 33–56.
13. Stout, *Sociopath*, 6.

diagnosed with a known scourge such as colon cancer."[14] Whether or not there is precisely one sociopath in every twenty-five citizens, Stout's statistic suggests that the existence of the sociopath poses a real social and moral problem. We are not raising moral issues about a rare phenomenon. We have experience with psycho-sociopaths, whether we realize it or not.

In my own experience, I have encountered various psycho-sociopaths, primarily college students and persons in professional careers. My realization that I was in the presence of such personalities goes back to early employment as an activity therapist working with patients in an Illinois state mental research hospital, some of whom were diagnosed as having "antisocial personality disorders," that is, as psycho-sociopaths.[15] I have clear memories of these patients and the file accounts of the incidents leading to their hospital admission. It is rare for psycho-sociopathic persons to enter mental treatment. They did then and do now make up only the smallest percentage of persons undergoing such treatment.

Much of the literature on psycho-sociopaths concentrates on describing the characteristics of the disorder as derived from case studies. The basic features of such persons are put forth in Cleckley's original clinical profile. I will mention several of the most striking ones that remain constant in the literature and that, in fact, accord with my own experience. The sociopath or psychopath lies, without concern for whether his falsehoods will be found out. When confronted by others for having told them a lie, he responds with a blank stare, a non-reaction, puzzled as to why his lie matters to them. The psycho-sociopath also, from time to time, will drift into telling an elaborate tale that features himself as the hero, overcoming various adversities and attaining extraordinary achievements. The tale may take on nearly mythic proportions and is presented so naturally that listeners at the time are impressed and astonished by it, and thus impressed by the person relating it. After an interval, however, and on reflection, listeners may realize how preposterous the tale was by which they were taken in. Normal persons do not tell tales of this order about themselves. On analysis, the listeners realize that there were inconsistencies and gaps in what was told, so that what it relates never could have happened. As far as the psycho-sociopath is concerned, however, the tale has served its purpose, and he has passed on to other things, unconcerned whether or not his tale has ultimately been believed.

The psycho-sociopath is usually intelligent and can convey much superficial charm. Above all, he is completely confident in his abilities and he

---

14. Ibid., 8.

15. Ward et al., *Asylum Light*, pt. 2.

can very effectually convey this confidence to others, who will see him as an exceptionally able person. They may hire him for a position, trust him, and believe in him and the abilities of which he seems so fully assured. His comportment is free of the emotional impediments, distractions, peculiarities, and awkwardness found to some degree in most persons. There will be no clear oddities in his behavior. As Cleckley writes, "Everything about him is likely to suggest desirable and superior human qualities, a robust mental health."[16] The psycho-sociopath is an expert at first impressions, appearing as a truly polished and self-possessed individual, but if, over time, his powers of manipulation and control are challenged, he can respond with bouts of rage, lashing out at anyone who interferes with his plans and actions.

Psycho-sociopaths have an incapacity for love, which is a part of their general incapacity to engage in interpersonal relations. They are often skillful in pretending love and in simulating parental devotion to their children. They are incapable of feelings of intimacy but often engage in sexual promiscuity, characterized by dominance and control of their partners. "Sociopaths cannot love, by definition they do not *have* higher values, and they almost never feel comfortable in their own skins. They are loveless, amoral, and chronically bored, even the few who become rich and powerful."[17] The psycho-sociopath is easily bored because he has no inner life to cultivate, no concern with understanding or grasping himself as a person, no spiritual or intellectual values upon which to reflect. When he is not acting, controlling, or dominating there is nothing there. There is nothing behind or within the roles he enacts for himself. His being is nothingness.

What relieves boredom in the reflective person is imagination, the ability to allow the mind and spirit to roam its limits, guided by a sense of the aesthetic and intellectual ingenuity or wit. These powers flourish when the human being possesses what Aristotle understood as leisure. Without an external project to pursue the psycho-sociopath has time on his hands and is simply bored. The psycho-sociopath seems to have imagination in a certain restricted sense. He can make plans, initiate possible courses of action, and formulate strategies, all of which require the use of images and the ability to transcend the present. But imagination as productive of the reflective powers of inner life seems missing in the personality of the psycho-sociopath.

The psycho-sociopath can make up elaborate lies that require a power of the image that, as indicated earlier, approaches the power of myth, but these false narratives contain none of the intrinsic value of a literary

16. Cleckley, *Mask*, 339.
17. Stout, *Sociopath*, 188.

production. Art and ideas, for him, are not sources through which the self is brought back upon itself. For the psycho-sociopath they are more akin to instrumentalities that may be useful to frame or promote his aims or programs. The educated psycho-sociopath sees no value in a line of poetry quoted for its own sake and appreciated as reflecting some aspect of the human condition. If he quotes such a line it is only for its potential to support some action, not to support the human spirit. To the mind of the educated psycho-sociopath the distinction between literature and what is memorable from popular culture is not particularly important.

The psycho-sociopath, because of his absolute self-involvement, is prone to hypochondria: "Because his concerns and awareness are geared exclusively toward himself, the person without conscience sometimes lives in a torment of hypochondriac reactions that would make even the most fretful anxiety neurotic appear rational. Getting a paper cut is a major event, and a cold sore is the beginning of the end."[18] Without a soul, without an inside life, the psycho-sociopath has only his body to cultivate. A threat or perceived threat to his body is a major problem, a weakness. He must feel himself essentially vital and powerful, a presence to others.

Without an inner life, the psycho-sociopath lacks empathy. "Many of the characteristics displayed by psychopaths—especially their egocentricity, lack of remorse, shallow emotions, and deceitfulness—are closely associated with a profound lack of empathy (an inability to construct a mental and emotional 'facsimile' of another person). . . . The feelings of other people are of no concern to psychopaths."[19] Moral sentiment above all requires the capacity for empathy. If other persons are apprehended purely as means, as vehicles or modalities that must simply be understood to gain one's own ends, they can never themselves be apprehended as ends. For the psycho-sociopath there is nothing as such to be gained or learned from contact with another person. For the psycho-sociopath, self-knowledge is not a problem. Without empathy there is also no basis for humor or irony. The psycho-sociopath, like the mentally disturbed generally, has little capacity for these reactions to life's vicissitudes. The psycho-sociopath takes himself seriously and can see little of the irony or humor in human situations. He can be sophisticated, cynical, and ironical in a conventional manner in professional or intellectual conversation, but he lacks the openness of personality to respond to or command a true sense of humor. His world is at base a dead-serious world of control and manipulation, of posing and imitating, of

18. Ibid., 189.

19. Hare, *Conscience*, 44.

conveying an appearance of confidence to others in order to gain their support for his projects, which are ultimately to his and not their best interests.

Of Descartes' six primitive passions, "namely, wonder, love, hatred, desire, joy and sadness," described in his *Passions of the Soul*, the psycho-sociopath has none.[20] Of the specific passions that Descartes derives from these six, most are antithetical to the psycho-sociopath, such as humility, generosity, esteem of others, remorse, timidity, fear, pity, repentance, gratitude, indignation, shame, despair, and regret. Some of the negative passions and their opposites—such as vanity, anger, jealousy, derision—might seem to apply, but they do not. For example, vanity, which Descartes says is a vice, might seem to apply to the psycho-sociopath, but to be vain is to esteem one's self too highly and not to possess true generosity. The vice of vanity presupposes the ability to be generous, and it is this capacity that is violated when one becomes vain. The human soul must be capable of this moral opposition. We might regard the self-centeredness of the psycho-sociopath as vain or consider his hypochondria a kind of vanity, but that is only a way of speaking about the psycho-sociopath—he is not capable of vanity in Descartes' sense because he is not capable of gratitude, its opposite.

The psycho-sociopath, as mentioned above, may become angry when his plans are opposed, but this anger is more of a rage, a violent reaction. Anger as Descartes understands it is a moral reaction, "a kind of hatred or aversion that we have towards those who have done some evil or who have tried to harm not just anyone they happen to meet but us in particular."[21] Like any passion, anger is understood in moral terms, part of the reality of a soul that has the capacity to experience the tension of moral opposites.

The Mask of Sanity, the title of Cleckley's classic study, is apt because at any given moment the psycho-sociopath seems sane and successful; yet he has no life plan and ultimately fails because he has failed from the start to be a person. Cleckley says, "Considering a longitudinal section of his life, his behavior gives such an impression of gratuitous folly and nonsensical activity in such massive accumulation that it is hard to avoid the conclusion that here is the product of true madness—of madness in a sense quite as real as that conveyed to the imaginative layman by the terrible word *lunatic*."[22] Yet Cleckley was not certain that psychopathy could be properly classified as a disease because it has no apparent treatment or cure. As mentioned earlier, none has been discovered in the more than half a century since Cleckley wrote.

20. Descartes, *Passions*, in *The Philosophical Writings of Descartes*, 1:353.
21. Ibid., 1:399.
22. Cleckley, *Mask*, 364.

Stout writes, "The argument can easily be made that 'sociopathy' and 'antisocial personality disorder' and 'psychopathy' are misnomers, reflecting an unstable mix of ideas, and that the absence of conscience does not really make sense as a psychiatric category in the first place." And, she emphasizes, "it is crucial to note that all of the other psychiatric diagnoses (including narcissism) involve some amount of personal distress or misery for the individuals who suffer from them. Sociopathy stands alone as a 'disease' that causes no *dis-ease* for the person who has it, no subjective discomfort."[23]

If they are not of the criminally violent type, psycho-sociopaths, in comparison with persons afflicted with other mental disorders, seldom come to the attention of medical professionals for treatment. They do not see any need to seek such help and pass through the world damaging others around them. Psychopaths are apparently born and not made; they are a true human type, if a completely negative one. Hare concludes, "On balance, however, I can find no convincing evidence that psychopathy is the direct result of early social or environmental factors. (I realize that my opinion will be unacceptable to people who believe that virtually all adult antisocial behavior—from petty theft to mass murder—stems from early maltreatment or deprivation)."[24] Without a viable account of how psycho-sociopathy comes about, there is little reason to hold that a therapy can be devised. The moral issues raised by the reality of the psycho-sociopath are not resolved by the possibility in principle that the future may bring a more effective clinical response to such pathology. It is also possible that no progress will be made. Without question, the moral issues associated with psycho-sociopathy exist at present.

CONSCIENCE

All analyses of psycho-sociopathy emphasize the complete absence of conscience in such persons. This lack of conscience appears analogous to the lack of one of the senses with which one might be born; some persons are born tone-deaf, others are color-blind. Color-blind persons can learn to compensate, for example, by realizing that they see as grey what others see as red. This adjustment enables the color-blind person to stop at a red traffic light as effectively as persons who see it as red. But the permanently color-blind person will never see that color to which he or she is "blind." The power of conscience is simply not there in the internal sense of the

23. Stout, *Sociopath*, 12.
24. Hare, *Conscience*, 170.

psycho-sociopath. He has no sense of remorse, guilt, or empathy because these are seated in conscience.

Hegel, in the *Phenomenology of Spirit*, describes the dynamics of the development of conscience as the state of consciousness in which the self ceases to oscillate between self and world and achieves certainty of its own being: "as conscience, it [moral self-consciousness] is no longer this continual alternation of existence being placed in the Self, and *vice versa*; it knows that its *existence* as such is this pure certainty of itself."[25] The realization of conscience as present in the human self is a key step in self-knowledge that results most immediately in duty.[26] To engage in duty places the self in relation to other selves. Duty as a human activity presupposes moral sensibilities—remorse, empathy, and so forth. The sociopath has no sense of moral duty nor the self-insight required to assume duties to others.

Conscience has its roots in synderesis, which originates in medieval Latin, from Greek *syntērēsis*, "preservation." Synderesis is inborn knowledge of the primary principles of moral action. Synderesis enters Christian doctrine through Saint Jerome, to whom Thomas Aquinas refers in his discussion of conscience, in which he distinguishes between conscience and synderesis.[27] He regards synderesis as the grasp of the common and natural principles of moral order, and he regards conscience as the application of such knowledge to the particular and changing circumstances of life: "through conscience the knowledge of synderesis and of higher and lower reason are applied to the examination of a particular act."[28] The judgment of synderesis is universal in the sense that natural law is universal. Thus synderesis does not commit errors in its judgments. Error is possible in the act of conscience when it applies these universal principles, but these principles are not themselves subject to error.

The standard source in the history of modern ethics for the nature of conscience is the *Sermons* of Joseph Butler. Butler holds that in matters of morals or "obligations of virtue" we can appeal to "each particular person's heart and natural conscience: as the external senses are appealed to for the proof of things cognizable by them. . . . And as to these inward feelings themselves; that they are real, that man has in his nature passions and affections, can no more be questioned, than that he has external senses."[29] Butler regards *reflection* and *conscience* as synonyms. Conscience is a kind

25. Hegel, *Phenomenology*, 481.

26. Ibid., 383 and 392.

27. Aquinas, *Disputed Questions*, 319–20.

28. Ibid., 324.

29. Butler, *Sermons*, 209.

of inner cognition that is objective and interwoven with human nature. "But there is a superior principle of reflection or conscience in every man, which distinguishes between the internal principles of his heart, as well as his external actions: which passes judgment upon himself and them; pronounces determinately some actions to be in themselves just, right, good; others to be in themselves evil, wrong, unjust."[30] Butler considers the exercise of conscience to correspond to Saint Paul's claim in Romans that "men are *by nature a law to themselves*."[31] Butler holds that conscience is instilled in human nature by God, but he does allow that, although conscience cannot be wholly mistaken, to a certain degree it is liable to greater mistakes than the external senses.[32]

John Dewey, in *Theory of the Moral Life*, raises the question, "Is conscience a faculty of intuition independent of human experience, or is it a product and expression of experience?"[33] Aquinas and Butler regard synderesis and reflection or conscience as a standard of morality placed in human nature by God. It is independent of experience and not as such subject to error. Fallibility enters in the application of this standard in judgments formed in connection to particular circumstances. The rise of the social and behavioral sciences has given support to the fact that decisions of conscience are culturally and personally conditioned. Many of the edicts of conscience appear to be reflections of the earlier ethical training of an individual and are not universal. The conscience of one individual may support war and the conscience of another may produce fundamental objections to it. Yet determinations of conscience are recognized in law. The existence of conscience provides the ground necessary for ethical theory to formulate principles that can make moral judgments universal and hence objective.

The psycho-sociopath not only has no conscience, he has no character. Character, like conscience, requires an inner life, a need to seek an ideal grasp of selfhood that is in no sense the concern of the psycho-sociopath, nor can it be. Of the nature of character, William James observes: "I have often thought that the best way to define a man's character would be to seek out the particular mental or moral attitude in which, when it came upon him, he felt himself most deeply and intensely active and alive. At such moments there is a voice inside that speaks and says: 'This is the real me!'"[34]

30. Ibid., 213.

31. Ibid., 211. See Rom 2:14.

32. Butler, *Sermons*, 209.

33. Dewey, *Moral Life*, 21.

34. James, *Letters*, 199.

This feeling of the need to have character, to be something excellent in and of one's self that cannot be derived from one's external relations or power over others, is closed to the psycho-sociopath. Such an aspiration does not even occur to him. The psycho-sociopath is forever the administrator of the action, generating control and further control, completely oriented toward the external. When fatigue sets in, as it does in all human affairs, the psycho-sociopath faces only boredom. There is for him no withdrawal into the self and its cultivation.

How to resolve the problem of the dialectic of the subjective and objective in conscience is not at issue here. Regardless of how this problem in moral philosophy is approached, conscience is held to be a power distinctive of human being. The complete absence of conscience in a person is a serious matter and a threat to the coherence of human community. Hare says of such persons, "In some respects they are like the emotionless androids depicted in science fiction, unable to imagine what real humans experience."[35] The psycho-sociopath is a menace, an alien being in the midst of human society.

MORAL PHILOSOPHY AND THE RHETORICAL PRINCIPLE OF PRUDENCE

The moral issue of the existence of psycho-sociopaths must begin from the fact that, whether or not their disorder is a disease, there is no known cure and no means by which to bring such persons into the world of human beings. The human world is held together by the presence within it of moral feelings, empathy, and conscience. The reality of the psycho-sociopaths among us may be difficult to accept. We live in an age of political correctness, in which everyone is to be seen as equal, in which there is thought to be a means to adjust any aberrant behavior to the norm, in which caring for the welfare of others is a pervasive value. But as one reads the works of Cleckley, Hare, and Stout the evidence for psychopathy and their analyses of it are impressive. Add to this any personal encounters with individual psychopaths and one can see that the problem is real. We have become accustomed in moral theory to affirming some principles to be true of human beings without considering whether all persons have a common nature. There is no consideration as to whether there is a class of aliens within the human world for whom such principles have no meaning.

We could attempt tenaciously to deny the existence or importance of the psycho-sociopath and hope that this denial will make the psycho-sociopath

35. Hare, *Conscience*, 44.

go away. As C. S. Peirce shows, tenacity is one of the fundamental ways people respond to difficulty. Response to the reality of psycho-sociopaths among us is no exception.[36] After all, despite the existence of psycho-sociopaths, society seems to have been able to function and continues to do so, although some studies of psycho-sociopaths, such as that of Stout, point to such ruthless leaders as Hitler, Pol Pot, Idi Amin, or Romania's Nicolae Ceaușescu as examples of psycho-sociopaths who have done much damage to society.

If we look to the *Inferno* in Dante's *Divine Comedy* we find a picture of the damage that can be done to society by the psycho-sociopathic personality. The *Inferno* is a map of all the vices of humanity arranged in descending circles, passing from the upper circles, containing lust and gluttony, to the middle, involving avarice, anger, heresy, and violence, to the lowest circles, concerned with deceit and treachery.[37] The upper circles involve the body, the middle circles involve the emotions, and the lowest involve the use of the intellect. The lost souls on these lowest levels were in life sowers of discord, involved in treachery against guests and hosts and engaged in deceit against relatives and friends. The vices of the lowest circles are the worst vices because they do more than corrupt the body or violently disrupt the course of ordinary life. They destroy the human bonds of trust upon which the very fabric of society depends, and those who engage in such acts do so by means of premeditation. It is here, on Dante's circles eight and nine, that the psycho-sociopath operates. His actions may not bring down society at large unless he rises to the level of political power and becomes a figure on the stage of history, but his actions gnaw away at all that is human among humans.

If we do not take the route of denial or "do-nothingness," the first step is to recognize and come to know the nature of the psycho-sociopaths among us. As mentioned above, the literature repeatedly points out that few psycho-sociopaths come to the attention of those capable of clinical diagnosis. Stout writes, "Sociopaths are not few and far between. On the contrary they make up a significant portion of our population. . . . People without conscience experience emotions very differently from you and me, and they do not experience love at all, or any other kind of positive attachment to their fellow human beings. This deficit, which is hard even to ponder, reduces life to an endless game of attempted domination over other people. . . . At present sociopathy is 'incurable': furthermore, sociopaths never wish to

36. Peirce, "Fixation of Belief," 12–13.

37. Dante, *Divine Comedy*, 44 and 312.

be 'cured.' . . . These facts are difficult for most people to accept. They are offensive, non-egalitarian, and frightening."[38]

The psycho-sociopath poses two problems for the moral philosopher. First, in the formulation of moral principles it cannot be assumed that they apply to all persons. They can apply only to those persons who are not otherwise standard exceptions to moral responsibility and agency, as noted earlier, and who in some sense have a conscience, that is, who have the capacity to experience the world in moral terms. Second, where may any guidance be found by which to orient our behavior in relation to the psycho-sociopaths among us? We must protect ourselves from psycho-sociopaths, as we must protect ourselves from terrorists, and we must observe the laws and customs of society in so doing; but we cannot form friendships with psycho-sociopaths or put our trust in them. There are no altruistic acts we can perform in relation to them; rather, we must act always in terms of our own self-protection. We may have special obligations to animals, the environment, and so forth. But we have no special duties toward the psycho-sociopath except to act in such a way as to preserve our own well-being, property, and sanity (and, if possible, that of others).[39] Psycho-sociopaths who commit criminal acts under the law can be and are dealt with as criminals. The law and the courts make no exception of guilt for psycho-sociopaths as insane. Those whose actions are destructive of others and of institutions but who do not violate the law pose more subtle problems.

There are no categorical rules or moral laws to govern our conduct in relation to psycho-sociopaths. The need in moral philosophy to overcome the subjective status of judgments by conscience requires the rational universalization of moral precepts. Although by means of conscience every person is a law unto that person, this law must also claim objective status by being in accord with reason. The freedom of the individual is the self-determination achieved by the law of conscience expressed as a law of reason, that is, as a rational moral principle.

The effectiveness of acting in accord with moral principles within human community presupposes the existence of conscience in both the person who is acting and the person who is the recipient of the action. The recipient must apprehend the action in moral terms or at least be capable of so doing. If not, the action is ineffective in bringing forth for rational comprehension the moral nature of the matter-in-hand that has provoked the action. Whatever specific moral principle might govern such an action has no value for

38. Stout, *Sociopath*, 155–56.

39. See Stout's "Thirteen Rules for Dealing with Sociopaths in Everyday Life," in ibid., 155–62. See also Hare, *Conscience*, 207–13.

the psycho-sociopath because, lacking a conscience, he has no need for or interest in universalizing his actions to attain the moral assent of others, nor of regarding the actions of others in these terms. Rational moral principle or moral law requires recognition to be effective. Its invocation presumes a power to affect the conscience of the community of persons involved.

In regard to persons whose reason is greatly impaired, or those who are insane, or very young children, conscience and dedication to moral law engenders care. As mentioned earlier, we have a duty to care for such persons, to come to their aid and give comfort. But it is impossible in any meaningful way to care for the psycho-sociopath because he can derive no benefit or comfort from it. The psycho-sociopath perceives his position in the world as perfect. He requires no aid or comfort. He may, as Stout points out, solicit our feelings of pity by portraying himself as disadvantaged and put upon in various ways, but this is only an attempt to manipulate us more effectively.[40] Our pity has no human effect on him. We can say, with Cicero in *On Duties*, "Some people are men only in name, not in fact."[41]

Aristotle says that ordinary human beings benefit from their participation in things good in themselves in varying degrees, but persons who are incurably bad receive no such benefit. "The just things exist among those who share in the unqualifiedly good things and who have an excess or a deficiency of them. For some, there is no excess of these goods, for example, the gods, perhaps; for others—for the incurably bad—there is no beneficial portion of them but all of them do harm; and for still others, there is a beneficial portion up to a certain amount. On account of this, justice is something human."[42] There can be no just acts between those who are capable of participation in what is good and those who are truly incapable of such participation. How are we to act when the condition required for just acts does not exist? The source for the answer to this question lies, I think, in rhetoric and not in traditional ethical theory as based solely on logic.

If we turn from ethical theory to the methods of applied ethics to deal with the psycho-sociopath in moral terms, we find no obvious solution. The general procedure of the applied ethicist is to consider evidence and arguments for a particular issue pro and con. But, as pointed out earlier, there is no pro and con to the fact of the psycho-sociopath. There is no positive side for which to argue, no better or worse form of psycho-sociopathy.

To deal with the psycho-sociopath, my best suggestion is that we turn to prudence. This sense of prudence is not that of a substitute or second-rate

40. Stout, *Sociopath*, 107–9 and 160–61.
41. Cicero, *De officiis* 1.30.105.
42. Aristotle, *Ethics* 1137a.

way of responding to moral situations when we find ourselves unable to act in terms of fully moral, rational principles. Prudence in the classical and humanist rhetorical sense is not striving for the formulation of the moral law through the abstractive and universalizing power of reason. Instead, prudence depends upon grasping another sense of law—the sense in which any particular situation in human affairs can be approached jurisprudentially. The law as a human institution is a process of civil wisdom and teaches us how to proceed rationally in any particular situation. Prudence is the power to act judiciously in relation to any particular situation. It is at the same time the cultivation of virtue in human affairs. What guides prudent action is always a sense of the good, the right, and the reasonable.

As discussed in Part 1 of this work, prudent action is based on the interconnection among *sapientia* (wisdom), *eloquentia* (eloquence), and *prudentia* (prudence) as formulated by Cicero.[43] Any situation must be grasped first in terms of what it is. Then the whole of it must be put into words so it can be held before our reason. Once what is in question is so formulated we have a basis to act, by taking into account all that we have brought before us. The model for this threefold approach is the law, or the art of jurisprudence upon which law is based. Vico claims that there is no "art of jurisprudence" as an art separate from what is needed for the general concept of civil wisdom. As mentioned in chapter 1, he holds: "There is only one 'art' of prudence and this art is philosophy."[44] Vico intends philosophy here in the general Socratic sense, that of moral philosophy as an inquiry into the conduct of life and as a way of acting that makes no one the worse for knowing one—a principle much like the first precept of the Hippocratic oath: first do no harm.[45] Socrates' maxim to make no one the worse for knowing him is inverted by the psycho-sociopath. The psycho-sociopath makes everyone the worse for knowing him, and it becomes a means for the domination of others.

This sense of prudence, as acting in any particular situation by taking it on its own terms, requires a different sense of the universality of our actions than that which is done purely by our reason. The universalization required is based on the art of memory. Recall the claim of the Renaissance humanist, statesman, and historian Francesco Guicciardini concerning prudence, quoted earlier in this volume: "All that which has been in the past is at present and will be again in the future. But both the names and the faces of things change, so that he who does not have a good eye will not

---

43. Cicero, *De partitione oratoria* 22.76–79.

44. Vico, *Study Methods*, 48.

45. Hippocrates, "Oath" 299.

recognize them. Nor will he know how to grasp a norm of conduct or make a judgment by means of observation."[46]

The patterns of the psycho-sociopath, once observed and understood, repeat themselves. We need to impress them on our memory in order to be able to recognize them in the particular situation in which we find ourselves. Our prudence or practical wisdom is rooted in memory. This art of memory preserves us by always allowing us to remember who the psycho-sociopath is and to be aware of his presence and prepared to respond in accordance with such guidelines or rules as are given us by those most knowledgeable of the psycho-sociopathic personality.

Our behavior is ethical in dealing with the psycho-sociopath, not because we are able to produce specific moral rules that govern our actions but because we are able in our actions to preserve our human dignity through our prudence. To be successful the psycho-sociopath must affect our dignity by reducing us to means to his ends, such that in the process we reduce ourselves by becoming subject to his manipulation. Our dignity depends upon the ultimate counsel that Socrates gives on our own mortality—that no harm can come to a good person. The psycho-sociopath may affect our circumstances of life, but only if we allow him to diminish our psyche can he affect our humanity. By means of our memory and the prudence based upon it, we can make the psycho-sociopath visible. As long as he can maintain his invisibility, the psycho-sociopath can wield his power or potential power over us.

The existence of the psycho-sociopathic personality remains a reality and a paradox, standing as a strange exception to moral principles of any type yet as a figure that must be confronted by them, for the psycho-sociopath does indeed possess the ring of Gyges—unless we are willing to direct our attention to the real presence of the psycho-sociopath in human affairs.

46. Guicciardini, *Ricordi*, 131. My translation.

4

The Technological Person:
The Dominance of Desire

THE VACUITY OF THE PERSON

IN CONSIDERING THE TECHNOLOGICAL person as an agent of the non-moral we face a version of the human condition or human type that does not pose a threat to the tranquility and pursuit of our ordinary life as the terrorist and the psycho-sociopath do. The life of the technological person is ordinary life itself, in modern society. Terrorism and psycho-sociopathy are phenomena of the human world prior to the development of the modern world that take on particular form in the modern world, but the technological person arises as a new form of personhood along with the technological society as the distinctive form of modern society. The acts of the terrorist and the psycho-sociopath pose external dangers the modern citizen must face, and they try our ability to act prudently, but in facing these types our selfhood as such is not in jeopardy.

The technological person is a threat from within, a threat to our existence as human selves. The pressure that the technological human type places on the individual is to be felt at every turn in modern existence because that existence is itself completely technological. In the technological world the moral act becomes unnecessary. Once we are overcome by the technological sense of experience we are like the rhinos in Ionesco's play. We have achieved a type of existence in which individuality and the pursuit of self-knowledge is unimportant. The ability to act with prudence in human affairs is replaced with an ability to adapt to the certainty of the mass. How does this state of affairs come about? How are we to comprehend ourselves as existing in the technological society? For as Jacques Ellul, the analyst of the technological society, reminds us, no one escapes from technique. The technological society is a world of the non-moral, and because it is our world, a world so close to us, we must take an extended look at its details in order to bring it even partially into view. It is the world we confront when we attempt to revise the activity of moral philosophy and the individual pursuit of virtue and the ancient aim of happiness.

In his famous depiction of master and servant in the *Phenomenology of Spirit*, Hegel says, "Desire has reserved to itself the pure negating of the object and thereby its unalloyed feeling of self." The self gives its being over to desire (*Begierde*) in an effort to deny reality to the object and assert its own unqualified claim to be real. "But that is the reason why this satisfaction is only a fleeting one, for it lacks the side of objectivity and permanence." The self cannot maintain its own reality as something merely in itself. To have experience requires it to stand over and against something other that is truly there and is not simply a projection of its own subjectivity. "Work, on the other hand, is desire held in check, fleetingness staved off; in other words, work forms and shapes the thing." Work (*Arbeit*) is a way for desire to confront the object and experience it. Instead of hectically denying reality to the object, the seeming permanence and independence of the object may be mastered and reduced by making it a project of work.

Hegel continues: "The negative relation to the object becomes its *form* and something *permanent*, because it is precisely for the worker that the object has independence." The nature of the object and the nature of its permanence can be affected only through the process of actually working on it. The object cannot simply be negated or conquered by a passion. "This *negative* middle term or the formative *activity* is at the same time the individuality or pure being-for-self of consciousness which now, in the work outside of it, acquires an element of permanence." Without the self's relation to something other, its experience of its own reality is fleeting. It has only the strength of its moment of desire. Through work the self not only defines the form of the object but also defines its own activity and achieves a permanence in this activity.

Hegel concludes: "It is in this way, therefore, that consciousness, *qua* worker, comes to see in the independent being [of the object] its *own* independence." Consciousness now accepts the permanence of the object as a key to its own permanence or independence, and the self realizes that the object can be incorporated into its own existence by transforming the passion of desire into the power of work.[1]

This stage of consciousness is commonly referred to as that of the "Master-Slave," which is a rendering of Hegel's title "Herrschaft und Knechtschaft," of the *Herr* (master, mastership) and the *Knecht* (servant, servitude). The *Knecht* is not literally a slave (*Sklave*), but the word can have this meaning in a figurative sense (*knechten*, to enslave). In the struggle of self-consciousness the *Knecht* is bound in his whole existence to the Herr and is "enslaved." The *Knecht* is not an employee in any ordinary sense. The master is his lord to whom he is bound. In Hegel's struggle of selfhood, the servant-slave, the bondsman, comes off the better in the struggle and wins mastery over his own reality. The master is left hollow and defeated. This is because the master's self-identity depends upon his power over the bonded servant. The master's aim is the pleasure or enjoyment (*Genuss*) of the object through the servant's work on it. The servant discovers that although his reality is essential to the master, the master is not essential to the servant's selfhood. The servant's selfhood is realized through his work on the object. The master knows how to direct the work, but the servant actually knows how to do it, and he keeps this knowledge to himself in times of crisis.

Hegel's metaphor of master-servant captures all forms of the struggle of selfhood in the world. It can be filled out in economic, sociological, psychological, historical, and philosophical terms. It has proved to be one of the richest metaphors in Hegel's thought and has been important for Marxian materialism as well as bourgeois social theory. The modern world is not shaped by either Marxian doctrine or capitalist economics. It is shaped by the logic that inheres in technological developments, what Jacques Ellul calls "the technological system" (*le système technicien*).[2] Ellul holds that capitalism and communism fundamentally disagree only on which system most adequately supports technology: "Communism's fundamental criticism of capitalism is that financial capitalism checks technical progress that produces no profits."[3] Events of recent years have shown that the communists were wrong; capitalism is the better doctrinal match for technology. But systems of economics do not determine technological advance. They follow along after it and supply monetary structure to what operates by its own internal forces.

It is not possible to think of a reformulation of philosophical thought and moral philosophy on humanist principles apart from an understanding

1. Hegel, *Phenomenology*, 148–49.
2. Ellul, *Technological System*, chap. 4.
3. Ellul, *Technological Society*, 81.

of the actual structure of modern life, which has been produced by a dedication to the desire to control the object and all that is in the world. It is literally a world of means without ends apart from the means. Technological society is not a choice; it develops in history. But it is grounded in a structure of the human self. What in the nature of the human makes technology possible? The immediate answer is that the human is not only *homo sapiens* but also *homo faber*. Distinctive to the human being is tool manufacture and tool use. Tools are the essence of work. Toolmaking and use are not engaged in only by the human animal, as was once thought, but are found among nonhuman animals. The Promethean gift, not of fire itself but of the tool, is wider than once thought.

Technological society is not merely a vast panorama of tool use, differing in degree of magnitude from primordial and early tool use and traditional mechanical processes. Technological society comes about with the first uses of machines as means of production in Europe in the 1750s. Marx says that John Wyatt began the Industrial Revolution in 1735 with the production of his spinning machine and that this beginning took place "without a word."[4] To describe this new form of society, I will use the terms *technique* and *technology* interchangeably. English does not have an exact counterpart for the German *die Technik*, French *le technique*, and Italian *la tecnica*. Literally, the word *technology* designates only the study of technique, not technique itself.

Technological society, which is modern society, differs in kind, not degree, from traditional forms of human society. Ellul makes an important distinction between the "technical operation" (*l'opération technique*) and the "technical phenomenon" (*le phénomène technique*).[5] Technical operation is what we commonly understand as tool use; it is nothing more than the use of means to accomplish something. Every operation in any traditional society involves technique or the means to accomplish something. Society becomes "technological" when technique becomes an object for "rational judgment," when a concern for the "one best means" is introduced. With the introduction of rational judgment, the question immediately is asked, concerning any means: is it the best means? Can it be improved? What was a matter of tradition, individual genius, and social evolution is now rationally interrogated as to whether it is the one best means. Everything in the technological society is constantly replaced, improved in a cult of the new.

To the direct application of rational judgment is added the intervention of "consciousness." Not only is any means judged in terms of its

4. Marx, *Capital*, chap. 13.
5. Ellul, *Technological Society*, 19–21.

possibilities for improvement, but a consciousness of technique is built up so that techniques in one field of endeavor may hold clues to their possible transference into other fields of activity. A second question is added to the question of the one best means: Where else might this means, perhaps with modification, be applied? Everyone becomes involved and concerned with the possibilities of technique. In the technological society everyone is fascinated with performance, whether it be of household appliances, gadgets, computer programs, electronic devices of all kinds, sound systems, communication, or spacecraft.

The suggestion box is everywhere. The worker is expected not simply to perform his work but also to participate in its efficiency. This is true for the consumer, who is constantly polled concerning his satisfaction with a product or service and its possible improvement. Evaluation cards to be filled out by the customer are placed on the tables of chain restaurants, in hotel rooms, car dealerships, and so forth. Course evaluation forms are filled out at the end of the term by each student in all university courses. The point is twofold: the information gained may be of some actual use, but more important is the continual engagement of the worker and consumer in the process of improvement itself.

Technical consciousness accounts for the rapid and far-flung expansion of technique in all areas of life, including forms of managerial organization, techniques of human relationship and self-improvement, and devices for entertainment, pleasure, and communication. No human activity escapes the "technical imperative." Nothing counts in society unless it is subject to technical formation. "The computer is down" is the equivalent of *Geworfenheit* ("thrownness"). We are "thrown" into conditions and must wait until the computer "comes up" for any activity to go forward. When it comes up, there is light again.

Technology is rooted in desire, in the primordial struggle of the self to be something. The struggle of self-consciousness that divides itself into master- and servant-selves is a struggle for the self to be real, to emerge in the world as different from the object. The consciousness that has mastered the world of objects attempts to master the new object of the self through force (*Kraft*). This produces the two selves. The self is born through fear (*Furcht*). The master fears that he may be nothing and requires the recognition (*Anerkennen*) of the bonded servant to verify his existence. The servant fears that he may be reduced to an object by the master's domination. The servant, as related above, discovers that he has the unique possibility to realize his self-identity in the activity of work. Through work he comes to be the master of the object; he comes into being as its permanent other.

The struggle between the master and the servant is a life-and-death struggle. When the servant survives by discovering work, he leaves the master with the problem of claiming his own reality. The master knows he is not real but can find no solution. Hegel says that he who does not play out this struggle to the end may simply become a person (*Person*): "The individual who has not risked his life may well be recognized as a *person*, but he has not attained to the truth of this recognition as an independent self-consciousness."[6] Hegel says, "To describe an individual as a 'person' is an expression of contempt."[7]

A person is a failed self. A person is someone without character, that is, someone who has not forged the self as an inner form of his being and is a self only on the surface. No matter what happens, anyone can claim personhood; selfhood is another matter. It is not by accident that the idea of "person" claims constant attention in technological life. "Persons" have rights. The tireless claims to the status of victim and to rights of every conceivable sort are based in the person's quest to fill up a reality that is all surface. The phenomenon of entitlement is based in the phenomenon of the person. Technological life's quest for certainty and "fullness" is driven by its *horror vacui*.

Hegel's phenomenology of spirit is not a series of inductive generalizations from history arranged as a progression of stages of consciousness. It is a "science of the experience of consciousness" in which the structure of each form of human consciousness is articulated directly from human experience and in which each form is placed within the dialectical order of the whole of consciousness. The forms of human consciousness that Hegel delineates appear in various periods of human history. In the *Phenomenology of Spirit* Hegel suggests this by referring to historical periods that illuminate various stages of consciousness. To understand history historically is the task of the historian, who considers events in terms of their ideational, material, social, and political causes. To understand history philosophically requires finding the particular phenomenon of consciousness that underlies any historical period. Any configuration of historical life is a consequence of its ground in the human itself. Human history is always derivative of the human. We may look within Hegel's book to find what fundamental feature of the human underlies our historical condition.

6. Hegel, *Phenomenology*, 114.

7. Ibid., 292.

TECHNOLOGICAL DESIRE

We live in a technological age. The form of modern society is technological. The key is given in Bacon's famous assertion: "Human knowledge and human power meet in one; for where the cause is not known the effect cannot be produced. Nature to be commanded must be obeyed; and that which in contemplation is as the cause is in operation as the rule."[8] Bacon's "new instrument" (*novum organum*) is a means for power over nature, a means for the self as knower to master the object known. The essence of modern thinking is captured in Bacon's statement. The ways of nature are to be understood in order that the knower can have his way with nature. We obey nature in order to command nature: "*Natura enim non nisi parendo vincitur.*" The cause of the instrumentality of knowledge is the passion of desire.

Descartes defines desire as an "agitation of the soul caused by the spirits, which disposes the soul to wish, in the future, for the things it represents to itself as agreeable."[9] We desire to command nature for our needs and, further, to do so for our own enjoyment, which, if pursued, will lead us to the production of luxury. As mentioned earlier, Vico says, "Men first feel necessity, then look for utility, next attend to comfort, still later amuse themselves with pleasure, thence grow dissolute in luxury, and finally go mad and waste their substance."[10] Rousseau says, "Luxury rarely develops without the sciences and arts, and they never develop without it."[11] Desire, if pursued as a pure passion unconnected to eros, ends in the cultivation of luxury. Eros is another matter, for it is classically a drive toward the good and it is properly tempered by piety.

Hegel says that the master's pure pursuit of desire fails to allow him to conquer the independence of the object directly and make it a thing existing solely for his own enjoyment. He says, "Desire failed to do this because of the thing's independence; but the master, who has interposed the servant between it and himself, takes to himself only the dependent aspect of the thing and has the pure enjoyment of it. The aspect of its independence he leaves to the servant, who works on it."[12] Our relationship to technology is a relationship of selves. The technological system is an alter ego. We, the egos of the technological society, occupy the place of the master in Hegel's picture of the primordial struggle of self-consciousness.

8. Bacon, *Novum Organum*, in *Works of Francis Bacon*, 4:47.

9. Descartes, *Passions of the Soul*, in *The Philosophical Writings of Descartes*, 1:358.

10. Vico, *New Science*, 78.

11. Rousseau, *First and Second Discourses*, 50.

12. Hegel, *Phenomenology*, 116.

Technique, the new instrument, fulfills the function of Hegel's servant, working on the object and confronting its independence. Technique offers up the world to us as a thing for our enjoyment. We believe we control technique and that it controls the world. The new instrument is more than Bacon could ever imagine. It is not simply a new logic of thought; technique is a new way of putting thought into action, so that nature is not only obeyed but is transformed into a thing that willingly fulfills our desire. Through technique the world will become what we wish it to be. It is not an accident that in the early development of household appliances they were advertised as "mechanical servants."[13] The image of the servant persists in the world of the personal computer and associated electronic devices. The computer enters the household as a servant of our personal informational needs. We now have a servant not only of the body but of the brain.

Technique stands in the place of the servant-self, there to do our bidding, and we mistakenly think technique can be directed according to our choice: "Technology is a means at our disposal and we must decide whether to use it for good or for ill." How often do we hear such nonsense? Every day, in one form or another. It is the "bad faith" (*mauvaise foi*) of ourselves as masters. We lie to ourselves, saying that means are a matter of choice, when in fact in the technological society all choice is made through the alternatives available in the technical system. The master quickly becomes dependent upon the servant of technical means.

The enjoyment and in fact the master's own reality is dependent upon the servant who appears to be at his control. But the choices the master may make are dependent upon those made possible by the servant. These are given as a result of the servant's work on the object. The servant defines his own choices in terms of the ongoing process of his work. When the servant discovers the object as work, the life-and-death struggle is over. The master is no longer a threat; the master's ability to fulfill his desire and prove the reality of his masterhood depends upon his uneasy reliance on the servant's work. The problem any administrator has is with his own reality; all other problems are within his power to solve.

When the life-and-death struggle is modified in the above way, the master ceases to be a lord and the servant a bondsman. The master becomes an administrator of the servant's activity, and in so doing the master becomes a *person*, in Hegel's sense of one who has avoided the full risk of being in the struggle, who has not "stared the negative in the face." The technological person feels dehumanized. This common anxiety of feeling dehumanized verifies that technique is our alter ego. The technical is our

13. Giedion, *Mechanization Takes Command*, pt. 6.

constant environment; it is the *Umwelt* of the human organism. The question of dehumanization goes deeper. The technological world is dehumanizing because there is no technique of the human, of being human. There is no technique for self-knowledge, the knowledge of the self as self, which is the basis of civil wisdom and moral philosophy. Wherever the self looks, it encounters itself only as *homo faber*, the self acting on the thing as object or on itself as object.

What Descartes could only imagine, we encounter as actors in the technological society. Descartes asks, when he looks out a window at men crossing the square, "Do I see any more than hats and coats which could conceal automatons?"[14] Today there is nothing remarkable about the possibility of automatons or of computerized brains. The technological world is full of automation. In Descartes' dialogue *The Search for Truth*, Eudoxus says, "I shall lay before your eyes the works of men involving corporeal things. After causing you to wonder at the most powerful machines, the most unusual automatons, the most impressive illusions and the most subtle tricks that human ingenuity can devise, I shall reveal to you the secrets behind them, which are so simple and straightforward that you will no longer have reason to wonder at anything made by the hands of men."[15] In the technological world everything is possible. Thought, reduced to method and applied to the object as instrument, the union of rationalism and empiricism, puts technique into the "hands of men," and technique takes on a life of its own.

THE TECHNOLOGICAL SOCIETY

The sense in which technique rules the modern age is captured in the original French title of Ellul's major work, *La technique ou l'enjeu du siècle* (1954), known in English as *The Technological Society* (1964).[16] This title is literally "technique, or the stake of the century." The use of the word *enjeu*—a term associated with gaming tables and meaning a stake, wager, money placed at risk in a game of chance—implies that human society has gambled all on one phenomenon: *technique*. The stake for this wager, accumulated over the second half of the eighteenth century and throughout the nineteenth, has been directly wagered in the twentieth century and continued into the twenty-first. The results of the wager will determine what is to come in the future. What we have *en-jeu*, "in-game," is our cultural, economic,

14. Descartes, *Meditations*, in *Philosophical Writings of Descartes*, 2:21.

15. Descartes, *Search for Truth*, in *Philosophical Writings of Descartes*, 2:405.

16. Ellul, *Technological Bluff*, xi–xii, reports that his French title was influenced by the publisher.

political, and personal lives. We have risked them totally on the single factor of technique.

This wager is reminiscent of another French thinker's device: Pascal's famous wager argument concerning the existence of God. Here, the individual in the deep solitude of his spirit and will can know nothing for certain of the existence or nonexistence of the deity. Pascal says, "I am forced to wager, and I am not free" (*On me force à parier, et je ne suis pas en liberté*).[17] The technological citizens are in this position: they must stake all they have as humans without any way to know the actual value of the wager they have made (for they are wagering all that there is) or to predict the outcome (for the odds are beyond calculation). As in Pascal's wager, the technological society always offers a choice without a choice.

Ellul defines technique as the "totality of methods rationally arrived at and having absolute efficiency (for a given stage of development) in every field of human activity. Its characteristics are new; the technique of the present has no common measure with that of the past."[18] Technique is the reduction of all human needs, wishes, and actions to means. All fields of human activity come together in an "ensemble of means." The employment of means is governed by the constant drive for the "one best means." Technique in Ellul's sense is not only the means by which man accomplishes the production of goods and the mastery of the material world, it is also the means whereby man produces forms of social organization of all types and at all levels and whereby the individual seeks to control and improve the forces of his own personality.

A life of means is in principle a life in which the traditional forces of fortune and fate are brought under control or eliminated. The wager of the century offers us the managed world, the managerial life, and, for ourselves as individuals, therapy, support groups, and self-help programs. All of these are part of the doctrine of political correctness, which reshapes the individual into a means such that the individual's eccentricities disappear into mass life. "Technique integrates everything. It avoids shock and sensational events. . . . When technique enters into every area of life, including the human, it ceases to be external to man and becomes his very substance."[19] Technique is the medium of modern existence. "Technique has only one principle: efficient ordering."[20]

17. Pascal, *Pensées*, 121.
18. Ellul, *Technological Society*, xxv.
19. Ibid., 6.
20. Ibid., 110.

The conception of "efficient ordering" is rooted in Descartes' conception of a "method of rightly conducting one's reason and seeking the truth in the sciences." Descartes' conception of truth as method is the technician's circle of efficient ordering. The beginning point for a technique is some result already arrived at, one clearly and distinctly given by an earlier act of technical ordering. From this, by dividing the situation into its parts and proceeding step by step to work out what is desired, a new advance in efficient ordering is achieved. The efficiency of the process is guaranteed; the circle is closed by a final act of checking the work and correcting for any loose ends. What I will call the "technical circle" is Cartesianism in action in all areas of life, whether in machine production, electronic conveying of information, time-study organization of the motions of prison guards, cafeteria feeding of mental patients, or a step-by-step method for achieving successful human relationships. Inside technology is Descartes' method, the homunculus of rational madness.

No theory is applied in technique; technique recapitulates itself. The quest for the "one best means" in every field of human endeavor produces technical civilization. Such a civilization is governed by a technical imperative, a science of techniques progressively elaborated. "This science extends to greatly diverse areas; it ranges from the act of shaving to the act of organizing the landing in Normandy, or to cremating thousands of deportees."[21] There is no personal choice in the technical world. "There is no personal choice, in respect to magnitude, between, say, 3 and 4; 4 is greater than 3; this is a fact which has no personal reference. No one can change it or assert the contrary or personally escape it. Similarly, there is no choice between two technical methods. One of them asserts itself inescapably: its results are calculated, measured, obvious, and indisputable."[22] Once one is committed to a method there is no choice concerning the results. Rightly conducted, reason produces a truth that is the beginning point for the production of another truth. There is no choice between methods when one will yield the truth and the other will not. We are unable to flee from the *huis clos* of technical thought. There is no exit. Every "problematic situation" that occurs within technological life is a new opportunity for a technological solution. In fact, technology requires this.

The self as master is born in the realization that nature can be commanded. Real mastery requires a means. The self develops technique—the idea of work put into the hands of another agency held in bondage to the self. The agency in servitude that will allow the self to be free to enjoy the

21. Ibid., 21.
22. Ibid., 80.

world is the machine. The machine used as a means of production is the first embodiment of technique involving the principles of rational judgment and consciousness: the technical phenomenon. The machine is a process that, once set in motion, will produce a desired end with only incidental human intervention: the mechanical servant. The self now has, but does not realize that it has, another self. This is the human self that is tied to the machine.

A factory is itself a machine having both human and nonhuman parts. Human operators of the separate machines in a traditional factory are disposable once the principle of the machine is perfected. In the modern factory workers are replaced by automatons, which are more perfect than humans. The entire process is automated by the joining of mechanical systems with systems of electronic control: robotics. The human element is reduced to those who supervise the control panels and perform maintenance, some of which is also automated. The modern factory is its own closed world. The closed system of the factory applies not only to production from inert materials; the same principles apply to the production of chickens and animals as meat. Henry Ford is commonly credited with inventing the assembly line, but its origins go back much earlier, to the Cincinnati slaughterhouses of the 1800s, to such devices as the automatic hog-weighing apparatus used to process and pack meat.

The human self that was once physically tied to the machine as its incidental extension is now tied to the productive society in a wider sense. As a technological person moved to the "service industry," the former machine operator continues to require factory-produced goods. Now a producer not of goods but of services, he or she is also a consumer of goods. No one has been set free, no leisure gained. Consumerism is a duty of Kantian proportions, imposed by the very order of things. It is the second role of every producer. Consumerism involves schooling in waste. The fast-food meal bought at the counter is packaged as if ready for travel into outer space. It is to be consumed a few feet away and the packaging disposed of on exit in a matter of minutes. In the technological world everything is carefully produced as disposable. Packaging is immediate waste and is recycled, in a microcosm of the technical circle itself.

TECHNOLOGICAL EXISTENCE

Once the machine appeared in the 1750s as a means of production of goods, everything had to be understood in terms of the machine. La Mettrie's *L'homme machine* (1748) is the advance statement of the idea of the modern self.[23] Once the computer appears as a means of intellectual order and social organization, a repeat of this process occurs: everything must be understood in terms of the computer. This occurs in the philosophical debates concerning "artificial intelligence."[24]

The fear that he is nothing rides the back of the modern rational man. Karl Jaspers says modern man is haunted by the sense that something is behind him: "A dread of life perhaps unparalleled in its intensity is modern man's sinister companion."[25] It is not a fear of a specific danger. Because of this initial and absolute fear the self feels dehumanized in its work. The Russian philosopher Nicolas Berdyaev says that in the world of technics man "loses his own image and is dissolved into his component elements. Man as a whole being, as a creature centered within himself, disappears. . . . Man has disappeared; there remain only certain of his functions."[26] The fascination with the importance of the individual, coupled with the fascination with the possibility that we are nothing, dominate the modern personality.

A symptom of dread is the constant concern for comfort. No one is to be made uncomfortable in the educational process; no one is to hear unwanted speech or to "feel" that one is working in a "hostile environment." Everyone is entitled to a neutral existence. Anyone at any moment may require counseling or therapy or need "quality time." Nothing is to be endured for the sake of learning or wages. Another symptom of dread is the ever-present concern with prediction of the weather. In a society where the uncertainties of the weather are of little consequence for daily life, the weather is predicted over and over; the slightest changes are carefully and relentlessly reported.

Death in the technological society is confronted by life insurance and, if desired, cryonics. After the explosion of the Challenger space shuttle in 1986, the death of the astronauts was described as a "major malfunction." Technological man does not want to encounter his own phantom. In a society based on bringing certainty to the vicissitudes of individual life, death, the uncertain certainty, is an especially difficult presence. The modern funeral is a model of efficiency. The body is embalmed and made lifelike with cosmetics to produce a "memory image" for family and friends at the viewing. Funerals may be prepaid. The ceremony is brief and may be videotaped. There is no dignity for the technological citizen, even in death.

23. La Mettrie, *Man a Machine*, 59–76.

24. E.g., Graubard, *Artificial Intelligence Debate*, and Dreyfus, *What Computers Still Can't Do*.

25. Jaspers, *Man in the Modern Age*, 62.

26. Berdyaev, *Fate of Man*, 32–33.

The technical impulse is rooted in Hegel's depiction of desire as the primary passion in the formation of selfhood. This depiction can be connected to his portrait of modernity in the stage titled "The Spiritual Animal Kingdom and Humbug, or the Matter in Hand Itself" (*Das geistige Tierreich und der Betrug oder die Sache selbst*). The cult of the matter in hand, of self-absorption, which was the particular vice of German romanticism, is likely what Hegel had in mind as an immediate historical example of this type of consciousness. John Findlay has pointed out that this goes much further: "The American business executive, the nineteenth-century empire builder, the disinterestedly frightful Nazi, or the pure practitioner of scholarship or research" are also examples.[27] Executives, managers, empire builders, Nazis, professors—all are part of the great *ménagerie* or "spiritual zoo" that makes up technological life, which is dominated at every moment by engagement with the matter in hand.

Hegel says the kind of self involved in the world of the matter in hand is one that "is simply in a reciprocal relation with itself."[28] The spiritual animal kingdom, the *geistige Tierreich*, is a collection of human selves held together by a kind of general spirit or sense of things that is analogous to that which holds the animal kingdom together. The ideal of this world of selves is a diversity in which no real variance from the norm of diversity is tolerated. All of us are really the same.

Hegel says, "Just as in the case of indeterminate animal life, which breathes the breath of life, let us say, into the element of water, or air or earth, and within these again into more specific principles, steeping its entire nature in them, and yet keeping that nature under its own control, and preserving itself as a unity, in spite of the limitation imposed by the element, and remaining in the form of this particular organization the same general animal life."[29] The animal kingdom does not really mean anything in and of itself. It works toward no particular end, yet each of its forms of life is completely concerned with its own matter in hand—the performance of its own types of activity. There is no overall goal to the animal kingdom except to perpetuate itself. It is just the activity of its own form of activity. It is "a Nothing working towards Nothing."[30]

In this world there are no real goals. There is just the business itself to be attended. There are no ethical or teleological directions. There is nothing beyond the self's reciprocal relationship to itself, a nothing working away

27. Findlay, *Hegel*, 113.
28. Hegel, *Phenomenology*, 238.
29. Ibid.
30. Ibid., 239.

at nothing. The self is completely in its own work, its activity. There are no formulated goals toward which the work of all the individual selves point or toward which they are dedicated. What lies beyond their individuality is only the general spirit of things, a kind of medium through which they all relate but which does not function as an end or a goal. It is a system of internal relations.

Each pursues the particular thing of his or her choice and believes it to be his or her unique form of being. Everyone has a career. But all choices are really just variations on the thing at hand, just specific courses of action in a general medium of action. This corresponds to Marshall McLuhan's thesis, in *Understanding Media*, that "in operational and practical fact, the medium is the message."[31] The medium is not a medium of anything; there is no message, no goal or cause outside of it. There is just activity to be enjoyed, a world of luxury as action and the consumption of action.

All that the individual is engaged in are activities of one sort or another. In this field of activity that is modern life the constant talk of individual choice is simply *Betrügerei*, "humbuggery," a deceit of whistles and bells. All this individuality and working together are just deceptions. The individual can never really choose, because he cannot choose to act apart from the thing at hand. He must choose one cause or another as his work. The highest thing to say is "I am just doing my job."

An individual heroic act in any sphere of modern life is immediately denied as heroic by the person who did it. Instinctively, the technological person knows that the idea of the hero is anathema to the technological society. There also can never be true working together, because the individual, if he is not to be nothing, must cling to his cause—which is always the particular "mineness" he can work out in relation to the particular thing. In the technological society all persons are potential victims, because the activity of others can at any moment infringe on the egocentric activity of the individual. When individuals are not feeling victimized by others but are busy and active, they find themselves thrown together with strangers in the fields of their activity.

In a traditional society a band of hunters tracking a dangerous animal under dangerous conditions have common values as to the practical and cultural meaning of the animal, their own identity as hunters, and the place of their activity within the total scheme of things. They also must be fully aware of the virtues and weaknesses of each of their companions: who can be relied on to stand firm at a crucial moment of the animal's charge, who

31. McLuhan, *Understanding Media*, 23.

is the most skilled, who is the least courageous, whose judgment is the most wise.

Hegel says, "The distinction between a content, which is explicit *for* consciousness only *within consciousness itself*, and an intrinsic reality outside it, no longer exists."[32] In other words, nature as external to the individual makes no sense. Neither does it make sense for the individual to believe that he has a nature. Human nature makes no sense. Hegel says, "Accordingly, an individual cannot know what he [really] is until he has made himself a reality through action."[33] This is Hegel's statement of the principle of existentialism: existence precedes essence. In the world of the matter in hand, everyone is an existentialist; everyone makes his or her essence through his or her sphere of activity.

In a modern flight crew, complete strangers can be put together to operate an aircraft without any knowledge of each other's virtues or personality traits. All that is necessary is that they are fully trained and certified. If in an emergency the qualities of character or the special intelligence of the crew takes over, it is simply a fortunate element. Training provides a certainty of procedure that in principle replaces any need for shared values or self-knowledge. The work is held together by training and technique. Nothing more is needed.

Everyone is anxious, experiences dread, because activity is nothing working away at nothing. It is not possible to specify the end or goal of this activity, apart from the specific aim of some individual project. We cannot say what human activity as such means. It is nothing. The individual experiences his being as nothing. He is just his activity, just his project at hand—waiting on tables in the café or seducing his companion in off-hours. The deception here is continual self-deception because the self cannot say to itself what it is, apart from one of its roles. The technological human world, like the animal kingdom, is just a general field of activity, with itself as its own end. The self as merely the project at hand is not the self that makes itself a moral agent through self-narration, as described in chapter 1. In the self as moral agent, its making of its character is guided by virtue and the good. Its activity is teleic. The technological self is nothing more than a field of activity without a telos. Whatever role it settles on for itself in the technological society is different in kind from the decorum the self achieves in its role in the theater of the world. In the technological world all roles the self makes for itself are equal and without particular moral distinction.

---

32. Hegel, *Phenomenology*, 239–40.
33. Ibid., 240.

The existential doctrine of the self makes sense in the technological form of society and consciousness. The medium of the technological world is *technique*. All activity is held together by technique. Everything is a procedure to be found in manuals, from those instructing restaurant employees ("waitrons") on the procedures for good service to those instructing anyone on methods for successful sexual seduction, for sale in mall bookstores. Neither honest work nor eros is anywhere to be found. In the technological society all individuals are engaged in activity, and this activity is part of the general field of activity that is the technological society itself.

Technical procedure also becomes the medium of politics. Herbert Marcuse explains his concept of one-dimensional man: "In the medium of technology, culture, politics, and the economy merge into an omnipresent system which swallows up or repulses all alternatives."[34] Ellul says, "It was Lenin who established political technique. He did not succeed in formulating a complete set of principles for it, but from the beginning he attained a twofold result. Even a mediocre politician, by the application of the 'method,' was able to achieve a good average policy, to ward off catastrophes, and to assure a coherent political line."[35]

Contemporary politics is determined solely by the medium, by the newscast "sound bite" and the candidate's television commercials. While the individual is told continually that he should vote on the issues, none of them is ever truly explained, nor could it be. In a world of information and interviews, explanation and interpretation are rendered unnecessary and in fact are meaningless. The deceptions natural to politics in traditional society are transcended by the systematic ambiguities, the "doublespeak" and "bad faith" of politics in the technological society. In technological society, even the most intimate human behavior is understood as politics—sexual politics, the politics of the classroom, the politics of parenthood, or political correctness. Moral philosophy is replaced by ideologies of "social dynamics," and justice replaced by "social justice."

TECHNOLOGY AND MORALITY

In the technological society good and bad judgments make no sense. What makes sense is achievement, which can include the successful acquisition of victimhood in a particular area and the subsequent claim to special rights. The most pervasive right is that of the second chance, discussed earlier. This is the claim that no one need ever fail, because everyone deserves a second

34. Marcuse, *One-Dimensional Man*, xvi.
35. Ellul, *Technological Society*, 83.

chance. Hegel says, "In contrast with this unessential *quantitative* difference [in comparing one individual's work with another], 'good' and 'bad' would express an absolute difference; but here this is not in place. Whether something is held to be good or bad, it is in either case an action and an activity in which an individuality exhibits and expresses itself, and for that reason it is all good; and it would, strictly speaking, be impossible to say what 'badness' was supposed to be."[36] The individual "can experience only joy in himself."[37] He has no basis from which to judge himself in terms of good or bad. He is a performer. As he experiences himself in action he is happy with himself. The technician whistles while he works. He is in the El Dorado of action.

To the self in reciprocal relationship to itself, moral judgments make no sense. In the technological universe, which stands only in relationship to its own activity, moral judgments cannot make sense. To be a victim is not to achieve a moral standpoint; it is to attain an advantageous position from which claims on others can be made. The victim replaces the citizen. Ellul says, "Technique never observes the distinction between moral and immoral use. It tends, on the contrary, to create a completely independent technical morality. . . . Not even the moral conversion of the technicians could make a difference. At best, they would cease to be good technicians. This attitude [that technique could be used for good or ill purposes] supposes further that technique evolves with some end in view, and that this end is human good. Technique is totally irrelevant to this notion and pursues no end, professed or unprofessed."[38]

Purpose makes no sense to the self that is joyfully engaged in its own activity in a world that it feels to be at its command, despite its general feelings of dread. In the technological society the notions of nature or the external world make no sense because the entire object is felt to be at the disposal of technique. There is no independent world of nature. Moral judgments or moral ends are irrelevant because the object shows no resistance. There is nothing to oppose the self in its rational activity, that is, in its activity of using reason as an instrument, a means. In a world in which all is functional, the moral judgment makes no sense. There is only activity, and there is nothing beyond the circle of activity.

Although the technological society is a world in which there are no ethics and no true individuality, there is the continual claim of individuality as well as the constant presence of "rights talk." There is sustained emphasis on the individual. Each individual has his own cause, his own role, and his

36. Hegel, *Phenomenology*, 241.

37. Ibid., 242.

38. Ellul, *Technological Society*, 97.

own matter in hand. The television talk show is the forum in which individuals are asked to voice their opinions. The individuals involved range from prominent personalities to welfare mothers, fathers who withhold child support, child abusers, thieves, bigots, street gangs, transsexuals, sufferers with bizarre mental or physical disabilities—a geek show of the human spirit. They are all blended into the moment of the medium, each to manifest his or her role and give his or her opinion. All opinions given have been heard many times before. No individual thoughts are possible, nothing can be understood. The host of the talk show emphasizes that the show is there to help others who may have the same problem. In what way this could happen is never specified, nor could it be. The talk show is a grand day out at the spiritual zoo. It is a public confessional.

Everywhere there is talk of the individual, but nowhere is any true value placed on the individual. Hegel says, "There thus enters a play of individualities with one another in which each and all find themselves both deceiving and deceived."[39] Individuals feign interest in each other in an effort to promote themselves. Hegel says, "A consciousness that opens up a subject-matter soon learns that others hurry along like flies to freshly poured-out milk, and want to busy themselves with it; and they learn about that individual that he, too, is concerned with the subject-matter, not as an *object*, but as his *own* affair."[40] The individuals sense that they command no substantial reality in themselves. The idea of character is irrelevant to them, to their existence in the technological world in which what counts is their role, their career, their perversion, and their ability to command some attention from others.

Individuals are just role-playing, and they will play any role so as to seem successful and real to themselves. They will appear on national television and confess their innermost secrets and deeds to no purpose and for no identifiable reason except that it is expected that they make the moment successful for television. What television and all its extensions in the personal electronic media present us with is action, which goes by the name of information. But because information is continually changing, information is in fact just activity. Anything can be information; information is an intellectual infinite. The self is attuned to this because it is in itself only matter in hand.

Ellul says, of the status of rights of individuals in technological society: "Modern society is, in fact, conducted on the basis of purely technical considerations. But when men found themselves going counter to the human

39. Hegel, *Phenomenology*, 250.
40. Ibid., 251.

factor, they reintroduced—in an absurd way—all manner of moral theories related to the rights of man, the League of Nations, liberty, justice. None of that has any more importance than the ruffled sunshade of McCormick's first reaper. When these moral flourishes overly encumber technical progress, they are discarded—more or less speedily, with more or less ceremony, but with determination nonetheless. This is the state we are in today."[41]

In the spiritual animal kingdom, any doctrine of individuality or individual rights is a deception. No empire builder, disinterested Nazi, business executive, or researcher takes ethics or individual rights seriously. What really determines the nature of things is the medium through which everything takes place—technique, the matter in hand. Hegel says, "Rather is its nature such that its *being* is the *action* of the *single* individual and of all individuals and whose action is immediately *for others*, or is a 'matter in hand' and is such only as the action of *each* and *everyone*: the essence which is the essence of all beings, viz. *spiritual essence*. Consciousness learns that no one of these moments is *subject*, but rather gets dissolved in the *universal* 'matter in hand.'"[42]

The matter in hand, like technique, dominates the activity of the individual. No genuine sense of the self is possible. All theories of the self or of rights are just projects of thought, just matters in hand. We can expect, as part of the self-deception, the humbug, of this type of consciousness, the production of all sorts of theories of justice, applied ethics, doctrines of individual creativity, plans for world peace, studies of public policy, debates on moral issues. These are all just matters in hand. They are just so much research and talk that keep the individual engaged, that give concerned individuals their own versions of the universal matter in hand, which is engagement itself.

TECHNOLOGY AND CHOICE

Writers on technology believe that they must evaluate technology and its effects, offer solutions, and discuss choices. Their approach to technology is guided by the question of what is good about technology (nothing can be all bad) and how technology can best be used to maximize human choice (man is free). Such discussion is generally conducted without grounding what is said in a fully developed moral philosophy. As Ellul says, "Anybody doing that has simply no understanding of what technology is all about, and he will find lots of cheap consolations. And that is the most common error

41. Ellul, *Technological Society*, 74.
42. Hegel, *Phenomenology*, 251–52.

I find in practically all writings on technology. The authors wonder if we can change the use of the automobile, or if television has a bad effect, etc., but this is meaningless."[43] Philosophy of technology that proceeds in this fashion is meaningless because it is itself technical. It approaches questions as though no metaphysics of the human or any moral vision were required. Its moral discussions often reflect no more than what is already under discussion in the newspapers, which are themselves a form of media in the process of disappearing.

The typical reason for rejecting a systematic account of technology is that it is a monolithic vision of technology in which technical advance is not truly subject to human choice and in which no clear solutions to the limits of technique are advocated. Here is a statement typical of this standard objection, from a work in the field of philosophy of technology: "Such a monolithic vision of technology is of little use in any future reform of specific technical cycles. *It* does nothing. We are responsible, and need instead an individual response to each situation, one cognizant of the dangers observed in the whole."[44]

What, we might ask, would be of more use in reforming technical cycles than a total grasp of the role of technique in modern society and consciousness? What is the evidence that we stand before technological life as free agents of choice, so that all we need to do is act "responsibly," whatever that might mean? The notion of acting responsibly in this context is like the notion of being "authentic" rather than "inauthentic." There is no way to know when one has successfully achieved either responsibility or authenticity. Technology leaves the individual completely on his own; there is no common vision of civil wisdom, as there is in traditional societies.

Writers on technology always assure us that technology is not monolithic and that the solution to all problems involved in technology is a matter of choice. These two commonplaces keep philosophers of technology in business, in a manner analogous to the pro-and-con arguments that keep applied ethicists in business. Most work in philosophy of technology is centered on the discussion of technology and public policy—that is, on the consideration of some problematic aspect of various technologies (affecting the environment, energy, communication, and so on), and then the proposal of various possible responses. Such often overlap with applied ethics.

Over forty years ago, Alvin Toffler wrote a best-selling work, *Future Shock*, in which he speaks of "overchoice." Toffler says that many critics of the technological society regard it as a standardized society in which all will

---

43. Ellul, *Technological Society*, 107.
44. Rothenberg, *Hand's End*, 189.

become regimented and everyone will gradually but continually be brought into a mass life. He says, "Such predictions have spawned a generation of future-haters and technophobes, as one might expect. One of the most extreme of these is a French religious mystic, Jacques Ellul."[45] Toffler says that Ellul warns of an absence of choice but that, "ironically, the people of the future may suffer not from an absence of choice, but from a paralyzing surfeit of it."[46] His example is "Design-a-Mustang," one of the most popular models of automobile ever made. We can create any kind of Mustang we want. It is the individual's choice.

For Aristotle, choice requires that we must know what we are doing, that we must do it for its own sake, and that we choose voluntarily, as the result of a permanent disposition. Let us imagine Aristotle acquiring his Mustang. He must know what he is doing. He can at least say to himself that he is doing what he is doing. He must choose which basic Mustang he wishes and what options he wishes to have on it. The options seem like virtues. Then he must choose voluntarily. This is the most difficult part. To begin with, he is not certain why he is with the salesman, designing a Mustang. There was never a choice whether or not to have cars. Cars just appeared. Henry Ford, seeing with perfect clarity into the technical process, said, "History is bunk!"

It is not Aristotle down at the car dealership. It is modern man, thrown into the conditions of his technical existence. We are there with him in the car dealer's world, about to emerge as the owner of our new Mustang or some other model with our complete set of mass options. Choices have been made; it has been a lesson in choice. This is what choice means within the technological framework of modern life: to consider one's options in any situation. For technology to be kept on the right course, Toffler suggests an ombudsman: "One step in the right direction would be to create a techno-logical ombudsman—a public agency charged with receiving, investigating, and acting on complaints having to do with the irresponsible application of technology."[47] I like to imagine Aristotle waiting for the office to open so he can consult his state's Lemon Law, which would further his experience of choice.

Moral choice as conceived by the practicing applied ethicist can now be understood: it is a projection of what has happened at the car dealership. We have an idea of what we want. Then we must balance the various factors and make a decision (in medical ethics this is spoken of in terms of balancing

---

45. Toffler, *Future Shock*, 263.

46. Ibid., 264.

47. Ibid., 442.

the costs off against the needs of society, the value of the individual, and so on). In making our decision we accept what initially was held out as the likely solution. The school of applied ethics is being run by the Ford Motor Company. It is as simple as that; in this ethical world, desire replaces virtue.

Desire is a valuable passion only when it is directed by intelligence and the will. But here desire—what we want—is the guiding force, and the will is what helps us to have patience in calculating the choices in relation to what is desired. We are not quite sure where the desire came from. Could it have been from the techniques of advertising to which we have been exposed? No one is more vulnerable to the technical process than the modern liberal intellectual, who is trained in critical thinking and who believes that he or she can exercise educated choice. In modern society this means reading *Consumer Reports*.

The real reason Ellul is a pariah for the theoreticians of technology is that technology cannot be criticized. Technology does not allow criticism of itself. Technological consciousness takes itself dead seriously; it has no sense of humor. The fool can play no role in it, for there is no other realm that it can see beyond itself to which the fool can point. Consciousness in the throes of desire cannot tolerate laughter any more than criticism or laughter can be tolerated in a moment of sexual lust. Ellul's real offense is to portray technology in an unseemly way. One cannot criticize technology any more than one can criticize the media. To criticize the media is always indirectly to criticize technological life. The media, while appearing tolerant of views on both sides of any issue, is in fact completely intolerant of criticism of itself. It responds to any criticism through its power, which is absolute. The media insists that it must be taken seriously. The media is the thought form of the technological society, and it finds nothing it does to be laughable—a sure sign that it is not human.

Jonathan Swift, I think, saw in advance much of what I have described. Swift is the first, in the "Voyage to Laputa" in *Gulliver's Travels* (1726) and in "A Digression in Praise of Digressions" in *A Tale of a Tub* (1697, 1710), to design and name a computer. *Compotus* (*computus*) goes back to the High Middle Ages, conceived as a science of exact chronology reckoned by rational means. Swift, the satirist, understood even more possibilities.

In the grand Academy of Lagado, Gulliver is ushered into a large room where a professor and a team of young students are operating a twenty-foot-square engine of knowledge, a contrivance that, with little bodily labor, "may write Books in Philosophy, Poetry, Politicks, Law, Mathematicks and Theology, without the least Assistance from Genius or Study." Swift includes a drawing of this great invention that will give "the World a compleat Body of all Arts and Sciences." In the digression in *A Tale of a Tub*, Swift says that "the Method of growing Wise, Learned, and *Sublime,* having become so regular an Affair, and so established in all its Forms," there is no longer anything left to explain such as would fill a whole volume. "This I am told by a very skillful *computer,* who hath given a full Demonstration of it from Rules of *Arithmetick.*"[48] Today reality defeats the satirist.

THE PHILOSOPHY OF TECHNOLOGY

The philosophy of technology as a special field of thought begins in the experience of World War I and the sense of mass life that followed from it. Philosophy of technology was from its beginnings a criticism of modern life, a realization that the development of society on a technological base brought with it not simply the social ills of industrialization, which by then were well known, but also certain requirements that it made of the human spirit. Technology involved a transformation of consciousness. This is the message of Karl Jaspers' *Man in the Modern Age* (1931), Lewis Mumford's *Technics and Civilization* (1934), Aldous Huxley's *Ends and Means* (1937), and Friedrich Jünger's *Die Perfektion der Technik* (1949 but written earlier). There are also Huxley's *Brave New World* (1932) and George Orwell's *Nineteen Eighty-Four* (1949). The threat of "Big Brother" has now been lost in the wonder of technological surveillance. The concepts of double-think and Newspeak, once so novel, are now simply accepted as part of modern speech: "War is peace," one says, or "Ignorance is strength" (so that a botched hostage rescue mission is announced as a "failed success" or a risky decision is considered in terms of its "deniability"). This outrageous use of language is a deformation of the human spirit; it is so much the norm that we do not hear its speech.

World War II further demonstrated the possibilities of mass organization and dedication to technical advance. Civilian populations experienced the mass order necessary to the success of modern warfare. This mass order, which was perceived in works on technology between the wars, was not simply a phenomenon of war; modern warfare is a dramatic embodiment of the general process of the managed life. Heidegger's "The Question Concerning Technology" (*Die Frage nach der Technik*) was given as a lecture in 1955. Ellul's *Technological Society,* as noted above, appeared in 1954, Siegfried Giedion's *Mechanization Takes Command* appeared in 1948, Pierre Ducassé's *Histoire des techniques* in 1945. Herbert Marcuse in *One-Dimensional Man* (1964) understood this transference from the mobilized population of modern warfare to life in peace time, what he calls the transformation of the

48. Swift, *Writings,* 155–59 and 338–39.

Warfare State into the Welfare State.[49] Ellul points out that in technological life "never before has so much been required of the human being. . . . Never before has the human race as a whole had to exert such efforts in its daily labors as it does today."[50]

The literature on technology of the last decades of the twentieth century has forgotten what was realized by the thinkers who first noticed that technology induced transformations in consciousness and social life. The philosophers of technology have forgotten to examine the insight summed up in Jaspers' comment: "When an attempt is made to render this inevitable institution absolute, there is a danger to the selfhood that the fundamental basis of mind may be destroyed."[51] Recent analysis of technology is dedicated instead to technological apologetics.[52] Once again philosophers have failed to go to school with the poets or to listen to them. They have missed what T. S. Eliot saw in order to write *The Waste Land* and "The Hollow Men" in the 1920s. They have missed Ezra Pound's "New Cantos" of the 1930s, where he says that the eighteenth-century *philosophes* employed all the arts of the Pharisees.[53] The Pharisees' arts of deception that accompany the technical arts are the Enlightenment's bluff, promising that reason can succeed in all its endeavors.

The philosophers of technology have missed Joyce's notice of this bluff in *Ulysses*: "It had better be stated here and now at the outset that the perverted transcendentalism to which Mr S. Dedalus' (Div. Scep.) contentions would appear to prove him pretty badly addicted runs directly counter to accepted scientific methods. Science, it cannot be too often repeated, deals with tangible phenomena. The man of science like the man in the street has to face hard-headed facts that cannot be blinked and explain them as best he can. There may be, it is true, some questions which science cannot answer—at present—such as the first problem submitted by Mr L. Bloom (Pubb. Canv.) regarding the future determination of sex."[54]

They have missed Henry Miller's vision, in *The World of Sex*, that "a new world is in the making, a new type of man is in the bud. . . . The body, of course, has long ceased to be the temple of the spirit. It is thus that man dies to the world—and to the Creator. In the course of disintegration, a process

49. Marcuse, *One-Dimensional Man*, 19.

50. Ellul, *Technological Society*, 319.

51. Jaspers, *Man in the Modern Age*, 123.

52. E.g., Floorman, *Existential Pleasures of Engineering*; Borgmann, *Technology*; Jonas, *Imperative of Responsibility*; Ihde, *Technology and the Life World*; Winner, *Whale and the Reactor*; Rapp, *Analytical Philosophy of Technology*.

53. Pound, *Cantos*, 161.

54. Joyce, *Ulysses*, 341.

which may go on for centuries, life loses all significance. An unearthly activity, manifested with equal ferocity in the pursuits of scholars, thinkers, men of science as in the doings of militarists, politicians and plunderers, screens the ever-waning presence of the living flame. This abnormal activity is itself the sign of approaching death."[55] Eliot sees this point when he writes that the world will end with a whimper, and Pound declares it should be a bang.[56]

In "Form und Technik" (1930) Cassirer wrote, "Man stands now by himself at that great turning point of his fate and his knowledge that Greek myth portrayed in the form of *Prometheus*. The fear of demons and gods is confronted by titanic pride and titanic consciousness of freedom. The divine fire is stolen from its immortal place and established in the domain of the human, in man's home and hearth."[57] Technology is a symbolic form that is understandable as one form alongside others whereby man as *animal symbolicum* creates cultural life.[58] Other forms are myth and religion, language, morals, economics, law, art, history, and science. Every organism has a "reactor system" and an "effector system," a way of responding and a way of acting. The human organism has in addition to these a "symbolic system"— the ability through images, words, and numbers to transform organic life into cultural life.

Each organism exists in terms of a particular *Umwelt*, an "environment," a surrounding world. The world of the sea urchin is full of "sea urchin things," and the world of the fly is full of "fly things."[59] The world of the human being is full of "symbolic things." The immediate flow in sense impressions can, by the human, be fixed and mediated through the power of the symbol so that what is sensed is the result of "finding again" (*wiederfinden*) in the symbol—in the image, the word or the formula.[60] The human never exists outside its circle of culture. All human experience, consciousness, and knowledge occur within the various powers of the symbolic process that are writ large in the basic forms of human culture. In the best of times, in a golden age, these forms are in balance and harmony, as with Heraclitus's bow and lyre.

The unique task of philosophy is to promote an understanding of all the forms as interrelated and to promote intellectually the ideal of their harmony. But intrinsic to each symbolic form is a drive to dominate all of the

55. Miller, *World of Sex*, 60–61.

56. Eliot, "Hollow Men," 80; Pound, *Cantos*, 74.

57. Cassirer, "Form und Technik," 66. My translation.

58. Cassirer, *Essay on Man*, 26.

59. Ibid., 23.

60. Cassirer, *Philosophy of Symbolic Forms*, 3:108 and 124.

cultural process. This is naturally true at the origin of human culture or the origin of any particular culture in which myth dominates, for all symbolic forms are originally mixed with myth and dialectically assert their independence from it. There is always an urge to return to myth, to the unity of the origin, just as in the individual there is always the wish to return to childhood, that state where, as Dylan Thomas says, time is yet to appear to the self.[61]

Instead, in the modern world we find ourselves exhausted in time, as Enrico Castelli describes in *Il tempo esaurito* (Exhausted time).[62] In the technical world of clocks and performance there is no respite, no duration in which the spirit can recover itself. Between desire and the satisfaction of desire there is only the action of the technological system; there is no duration in which examination and choice can be considered. In our age the symbolic form of technique has become successful in entering into all other forms of culture and structuring them in terms that are desirable for technical advance. How has this occurred?

Cassirer suggests the answer in *The Myth of the State* through an analysis of twentieth-century political myths.[63] The successful use of political myth by National Socialism is an example on a grand scale, but what is true of National Socialism in this regard is true of modernity in general. Ellul points out that the original theory of the concentration camp, "preventative detention" and "reeducation" (to remove the undesirable from society in order to adjust him to it), is the same as the modern theory of penology.[64] In the technological society prisons exist not for punishment but as means for managing a problematic part of society. Justice and punishment are irrelevant to crime in the technological society. The criminal, even if guilty of capital crimes, is incarcerated and released, to be with near surety incarcerated again, in a cycle.

The law becomes a form of instrumental order for embodying various moments of social ideology. The law loses its ancient connection with *ius* and becomes simply *lex*. The law has no connection with what human beings and the cosmos really are. Life in the technological society is in every sense lawless. Every individual in the society knows that should a crime be committed against him or his property, no justice will result; only the world of Franz Kafka will ensue—a series of unimaginable complications

61. Thomas, "Fern Hill," 195.

62. Castelli, *Il tempo esaurito*, 329 and 329n2.

63. Cassirer, *Myth of the State*, chap. 18. See also Cassirer, *Symbol, Myth, and Culture*, 233–67.

64. Ellul, *Technological Society*, 102.

that exist in their own cycle of justification. The courts are institutions of social management and legalistics, not a theater of justice.

MODERN POLITICS

Technology becomes the form of modern life by joining its powers of domination and fulfillment of human desire with the powers of myth. It does this first through politics. Modern politics exists by joining the mythic image and the mythic logic of the forces of good and evil with the techniques of communication: the media. Politicians are successful only by turning themselves into media images. They hold office by being constantly "informed." Ellul says in *The Political Illusion*, "Progress is to read newspapers."[65] Propaganda in the technical society is the media. Old-fashioned propaganda, in which deliberate lies were told to influence opinions against racial groups or social classes, has no power over the masses.[66]

Attitudes are formed in advertising by telling a truth in the form of an image. In these images appear the mystic light, the magical journey, the wise figure who provides knowledge needed for life's way (this can be, for example, in the form of the druggist who recommends a hemorrhoid preparation to a grateful customer), Mother Earth, the demon (the consumer is saved from a bad situation by a new product), the divine child, the divine maiden, and Tom Thumb or Hans Brinker (something or someone very small but capable of enormous beneficial effect), the hidden king, the hermaphrodite, the magic elixir. The themes of all the archetypes of Jung's "collective unconscious" are there. What in traditional societies are formed into the narratives of myths and fairy tales are met by the modern psyche point-blank in television commercials and magazine layouts.[67]

In the print media, as it is called, journalism has ceased to exist in the classic sense of informing the reader of who, what, where, when, how, and why. Only a small portion of any daily newspaper is taken up with reports of actual occurrences; all sorts of things are written about: food, women's issues, design, education, ideas, children's news, the arts, good living, the environment, and so on. What at one time was included in the Sunday supplements is now the daily newspaper. A crime, a political event, an accident is presented as a kind of impressionistic whole; the reader is left with few specific details of the event. The reader cannot know with any precision what actually happened. Only some broad indication of how or why a crime

65. Ellul, *Political Illusion*, 17.

66. Ellul, *Propaganda*, chap. 1.

67. Jung, *Two Essays on Analytical Psychology*, 100–123.

happened is given because there is no need to think through its specifics, especially why it occurred. Its basic significance is action reported. The print media imitates television. After watching the evening news the viewer finds it impossible to remember with any precision what was reported. During the newscast the impressions are vivid, but they do not become thoughts.

In the technological world art becomes a means for advertising. The patterns of Piet Mondrian's paintings, what he called "neoplasticism" (the use of blocks of primary colors marked off with lines of white and black), become patterns for fabrics. The unique arrangement of words in e. e. cummings' poetry becomes the key to layouts for magazine advertisements. Fragrances can be sold by joining images of intimacy with a voice speaking lines from Ernest Hemingway's *The Sun Also Rises* or D. H. Lawrence's *Lady Chatterley's Lover*. The first to see these possibilities was Walter Benjamin, in his "Das Kunstwerk im Zeitalter seiner technischen Reproduzierbarkeit" (The work of art in the age of "mechanical" reproduction).[68] It is unnecessary that the viewer have any idea of the source of the images or the language used. In the technological world, art and literature become effective instruments of the media but do not offer a critical perspective on human life, society, or technology itself. Anything can be included in the medium of technical consciousness.

In the technical world, what people have most in common are the images of television commercials. Every instructor in a classroom has a basis of common reference with his or her students, not by citing some work of literature, a painting, or a historical event that is part of traditional learning but by calling forth some part of a commercial. The individual eye has seen with complete precision just what the mass eye has seen and is ready to respond to its mention. History, science, morals, economics, and the law are not immune to the media.

We look into the *Wunderkammer* of television, and we find all of these forms of culture on display. There is the History Channel, on which dramatic moments of history are portrayed; undramatic moments are not. Television makes entertainment out of trials held all over the English-speaking world as well as dramatization of crimes and all forms of police work. There are programs on handling and investing money, and on the "business day." Every moral issue is handled time after time on talk shows, as mentioned above. If there is a discovery of great scientific and theoretical interest, scientists or intellectuals may be interviewed to explain, in the manner of sound bites, the nature of the discovery. There is no need to understand anything further; we have heard about it in much the same way as if we had seen a

68. Benjamin, "Das Kunstwerk," 136–69.

travel program on the Grand Canyon. It is not especially necessary to see the site itself. We know what it looks like. A visit to a historic site revolves around the film shown in the visitors' center. These examples will quickly become old, as would any examples that could be given; technological life and the media are in Plato's world of becoming. Technology is the cult of the new. It is impossible to talk about.

Politics is carried on by the logic of the millennium, that is, the logic of the continual announcement of the arrival of the apocalypse. Cassirer says, "Our modern political life has abruptly returned to forms which seemed to have been entirely forgotten. To be sure, we no longer have the primitive kind of sortilege, the divination by lot; we no longer observe the flight of birds nor do we inspect the entrails of slain animals. . . . Our modern politicians know very well that the great masses are much more easily moved by the force of imagination than by sheer physical force. And they have made ample use of this knowledge. The politician becomes a sort of public fortuneteller. Prophecy is an essential element in the new technique of rulership. The most improbable or even impossible promises are made; the millennium is predicted over and over again."[69]

The technological society exists by the logic of the millennium. The public, who has been deep into the quest for certainty of life and satisfaction of desires that technology provides, is periodically informed that there is irreparable damage to the ozone layer; that there is global warming and the possibility of a new ice age; that the rainforest is being depleted with unimaginable rapidity (this, for some reason, is a frequent topic of discussion in elementary schools, where it often brings children to tears and desperation); that there is a raw materials crisis; that there is an energy crisis; that the infrastructure of the utilities of large cities is deteriorating and may be too complex to repair; that there is overpopulation, pollution, multiple crises of the "environment" (whatever this term may mean); and that viruses for which there is no known cure are being released from the world's jungles, due to invasion of their ecosystems (the AIDS virus being but one example). The list only increases. It is technology's way of mobilizing an attitude of support and dependence from the individual. Each of these threats is simply a version of the apocalypse suddenly shown to the individual. The millennium is predicted over and over again.

The reality of the four horsemen of the apocalypse—famine, war, pestilence, and death—was once met with religious and communal values; these were the ways that the individual could face what could not be controlled. The advent of technological society has eliminated these forces of evil, or so

69. Cassirer, *Myth of the State*, 289.

it announces. But it brings up their existence in a drama of self-fulfillment. No new choices are introduced by raising the specter of disaster. These become opportunities for swearing new allegiance to technology. The solution is to discover new technologies that will correct and modify the harm either potentially or already caused by present technologies. In a cycle, the threatening technologies continue, and new corrective ones are added.

Technology is always doubling itself. This doubling up goes hand in hand with the "technological bluff."[70] This bluff is technology's claim, along with science, that it can offer a solution to all problems. It is the idea that "we're working on it," that nothing is beyond solution, that science marches on. It is also the claim that science and technology have done more at any moment than they actually have done, or of which they are capable. The promise of technology is to remove the division between culture and nature. Whatever part of nature that is left over as an independent force is covered by the technological bluff, which refers it to the agenda of the future and disguises the deficiencies of the present.

Ellul sees the technical phenomenon as having the property of *unicité* or *insécabilité*, that separate techniques form a whole. "It is common practice, for example, to deny the unity of the technical complex so as to be able to fasten one's hopes on one or another of its branches."[71] We need not go far to see what *unicité* means. We know that the production of goods, their marketing, their consumption, their raw materials all make up an interlocking system and that the actual production of goods requires workers who have undergone systems of education, training, and psychological conditioning and whose efforts are organized by layers of managerial order.

Technological life operates on the pleasure-pain principle. Work is pain, but not great pain; it is relieved by the coffee break, the lunch break, by company activities. The individual returns home, exhausted by time filled by performance of work. Pleasure is to eat a dinner of processed food while watching television—which at the same time will sell the viewer products and convey information. Or the evening may be spent searching for information on the Internet, which is the same as watching television. The individual is alone with the world. This loneliness may be "relieved" by electronic contact or "conversations" with absolute strangers and can include posting the most intimate images, declarations, and experiences for unlimited numbers of people to see and read.

Television is dominated by sports, information, situation comedies, soap operas, so-called reality shows, and talk shows. Modern sports are

70. Ellul, *Technological Bluff*, xv–xvi.
71. Ellul, *Technological Society*, 95.

panoramas of action; information is intellectual action; reality shows and talk shows are psychic and linguistic action; situation comedies and soap operas are instructional films on the nature of citizenship in the technological society. The individual is never portrayed as the master of his or her fate, but as thrown into conditions or emotions beyond his or her control. They establish ideal forms of human interaction to be imitated, both good and bad.

The function of the music hall, which originated during the Industrial Revolution to entertain workers massed in cities so that they could tolerate their hours at repetitive work, is handled by the media in contemporary electronic life. The technological life that originated in eighteenth-century Europe and America now overlays the earth. The Yanomamö, an isolated, completely primordial people discovered in the South American rainforest only a few decades ago, now wear T-shirts and have portable electronics. Like the perfect salesman, technology can enter any door with its products.

Ellul holds that technology involves the property of self-augmentation (*autoaccroissement*). He says, "On the whole, it is the principle of the combination of techniques which causes self-augmentation. Self-augmentation can be formulated in two laws: 1. *In a given civilization, technical progress is irreversible.* 2. *Technical progress tends to act, not according to an arithmetic, but according to a geometric progression.*"[72] Technical progress is irreversible because of the presence of rational judgment in the technical phenomenon, the choice always of the "one best means," the ideal of total efficiency. Technical progress acts in a geometric progression because of the factor of consciousness in which any technique, once established in one area of human endeavor, can leap great distances in a single bound and be applied and modified for use in a totally different area of experience. In "Travels in Hyperreality" Umberto Eco remarks on the phenomenon of "more" in American society: would you like "more coffee" (the bottomless cup); there is "more to come" (stay with the television program through its commercials, because there is more to come); "more flavor" (in a particular soft drink or coffee).[73]

Desire is governed always by "more"; nothing is ever enough. The Marquis de Sade in *Le philosophes dans le boudoir* describes the ideal state, in which desire in the form of sexual libertinage could function with perfect efficiency. He interrupts his characters in the middle of their magnificent lusts to consider the theoretical possibility that, in a utopia of libertinage, "various stations, cheerful, sanitary, spacious, properly furnished and in

72. Ibid., 89.
73. Eco, *Travels in Hyperreality*, 7–8.

every respect safe, will be erected in divers points in each city; in them all sexes, all ages, all creatures possible will be offered to the caprices of the libertines who shall come to divert themselves, and the most absolute subordination will be the rule of the individuals participating."[74]

For the technological citizen, libertinage is available as a method. *The Joy of Sex* promises "more sex"; in fact, its sequel is titled *More Joy of Sex* and is followed by *New Joy of Sex*. How different from the erotic formulations of Ovid's *Art of Love*, the metaphysics of the *Kama Sutra*, or the bodily wisdom of the *Perfumed Garden*! Desire, whether for sex or power, always has the logic of "more," and so does technology. As in the world of sexual seduction or corporate power, so in the world of technique—the individual lives in the world as in a menagerie of competing interests. Action has as its end more action; it does not have eros or purpose.

TECHNOLOGY, SCIENCE, AND LANGUAGE

Technology is often understood simply as applied science. There may have been a period in the late nineteenth and early twentieth centuries when this relationship between science and technology could be said to hold. That was the age of invention, in which single individuals with a rudimentary knowledge of scientific principles and some equipment could apply such principles in order to make discoveries. In this age of invention the most important invention was the idea of invention itself. Today any philosopher of science knows, as does any philosopher of technology, that scientific research requires great technological support from the development of new types of processes and instruments, computer systems, granting agencies, personnel techniques for organizing the work of assistants, techniques of publicity, and so on. Science and technology are not distinguishable. Science requires technology to function, and technological advance continually sets up new scientific possibilities. Although seeming to be auxiliary to science, technology has in fact always been the future of science. Cassirer's analysis of concept formation makes this clear.

Cassirer shows that the shift from Aristotelian-Scholastic physics to Galilean physics is tied to a shift in symbolism.[75] The fundamental category of Aristotelian thought is substance or being. The subject of a sentence reflects the substance or substratum to which the predicate refers. Physical nature is described by Aristotle through things and their properties. The shift from Aristotelian and Scholastic physics to Galilean physics depends

74. de Sade, *Justine*, 316–17.
75. Cassirer, "Influence of Language," 309–27.

upon replacing the symbols of language, with its subject and predicate structure, with the symbols of mathematics, with its notational and calculative structure.

We first meet with the distinction between primary and secondary qualities in Galileo's *Il saggiatore* (The assayer). What Aristotelian science regarded as the objective properties of things—heat, cold, bitter, sweet, red, blue—become only secondary qualities of physical nature. Cassirer says nature "is an open book legible to everyone. But in order to read this book we first have to learn the letters in which it is written. These letters are not the ordinary sense-data: the perceptions of heat or cold, of red or blue, and so on. The book of nature is written in mathematical characters, in points, lines, surfaces, numbers. By this postulate Galileo removed the keystone of Aristotelian physics."[76]

The shift in the symbols by which the book of nature can be read, which is first accomplished by Galileo, develops in modern science into what Cassirer calls the functional concept.[77] The shift is from the substance-concept (*Substanzbegriff*) to the function-concept (*Funktionsbegriff*). The propositional function is the model of the significative form of thinking (*Bedeutungsfunktion*). The propositional function $\Phi(x)$ is composed of two logically dissimilar factors that are yet held together in a bond. The universal element Φ can never be a member of the series represented by x, that is, $x_1, x_2, x_3,$ . . . In like manner the particular elements of the series $x_1, x_2, x_3,$ . . . can never be within the particular structure transformed into the universal element Φ, the principle of order of the series. This notion is absolutely simple, yet it holds the key for, among other things, the internal order of any form of symbolism. In the Aristotelian view of concept formation, the mind moves among particulars and articulates the property common to them. Physical events can be spoken about only in terms of generalized definitions.

The universalizing thrust of the concept has no power to connect the concept back to the particular event. In Galilean physics based on numbers and their formulas, the individual event can be followed in its motions and interactions with other events. Such notational thinking has the power at least in principle to adjust itself perfectly to the patterns of observable actions in nature. The power of the knower and the concept is greatly increased. But as a functional concept the object here is still known only through observation and calculation. Nature exists to be obeyed in order to be commanded. Nature is something independent of the knower. What I will call the technical concept emerges as a development of the functional

76. Ibid., 316.

77. Cassirer, *Philosophy of Symbolic Forms*, 3:281–314.

concept. It emerges because of the technical impulse that is grounded in desire to command the object more fully and to anticipate accurately and calculate its motions.

The technical concept takes up the notion that knowledge is power in the fullest sense. The technical concept does not bridge the relation between Φ and (x) by the adjustment of Φ to the series of observational independent particulars that are the x series. In the technical concept reality is taken in hand from the side of the knower. The knower devises a means to accomplish the connection between Φ and (x) of the functional concept. Through the power to grasp procedure, the relationship between the universal and the particular elements of this structure becomes wholly active. Through increased consciousness of technical procedure, the particular event is made to fit the law of the concept in a specific and workable fashion. This becomes the ensemble of means that is technological order.

Concept formation describes a way of thinking. Coupled to this is a way of speaking, of using language. The technological society requires a way of using language such that it follows the closed circle between the universal and the particular, between the knower and the known as dominated by the knower. This requires, in addition to what has been said above about language and images, the "humiliation of the word." It requires that the dialectical use of language be replaced with a form of procedural speech in the sphere of dealing with objects and with an imagistic speech in dealing with the human and cultural world.

Cassirer describes in *The Myth of the State* the creation of Nazi-Deutsch, of which even a dictionary could be made. Words in ordinary German were changed in meaning; for example, a sharp difference was made between *Siegfriede* and *Siegerfriede*: "*Sieg* means victory, *Friede* means peace; how can the combination of the two words produce entirely different meanings? Nevertheless we are told that, in modern German usage, there is all the difference in the world between the two terms. For a Siegfriede is a peace through German victory; whereas a Siegerfriede means the very opposite; it is used to denote a peace which would be dictated by the allied conquerors. It is the same with other terms."[78] At first it seems strange that technique can merge with what would seem to be its enemy, the mythic image. The basis of this merger is the I-Thou relation that each has with the object. Both technical desire and myth, each in its own way, approach the object as an alter ego. It is this immediate merging with the object that allows them so easily to form their bond, joining technical action with imagistic thinking.

78. Cassirer, *Myth of the State*, 283–84.

The constant redefinition of terms that refer to any human deviance from the standard is the resurgence of word-magic in technological life. The shift from *crippled* to *handicapped* to *disabled* to *physically challenged* to *differently abled*, and so forth, has within it the unspoken attitude that if the name for an infirmity is changed in language the actuality will somehow be improved, a medicine of words. No one is allowed to be simply blind, deaf, obese, retarded, or insane. Infirmities are accepted only as malfunctions that can be brought back to the norm, if not by procedures of modern medicine then through the politics of speech. The same is true of terms related to all social issues. Patients seeking treatment from psychiatrists or therapists are renamed *clients*, as if they were just seeking advice and not suffering from neurosis or emotional illness. This reform of language is one of the most evident effects of the intolerance by political correctness of the direct use of ordinary English.

All this is done in the belief that social advance will be accomplished in formulating a non-prejudicial speech and eliminating "old ways of thinking," or "Oldspeak." In *Nineteen Eighty-Four* Orwell says, "Newspeak is called *doublethink. . . . Doublethink* means the power of holding two contradictory beliefs in one's mind simultaneously, and accepting both of them."[79] The need for charity of spirit toward those less fortunate or those who live under injustice is made unnecessary by the act of progressive renaming. Human dignity is handed over to linguistic and social procedure. Mass life requires constant inclusion of any deviance from the normal, and this begins with the reform of language. Plain speech in which words are tied to objective conditions becomes impossible.

Words revert to word-magic when they become imagistic in the above way. In the technological world, language has been transformed to fit a world determined by technique joined to the mythical image. Ellul says, "Images are indispensable for the construction of the technological society. If we remained at the stage of verbal dialogue, inevitably we would be led to critical reflection. But images exclude criticism. The habit of living in this image-oriented world leads me to give up dialectical thought and criticism. It is so much easier to give up and let myself be carried along by the continually renewed wave of images. They provide me from moment to moment with exactly the amount of stimulus I need."[80] Dialectical speech presumes that there is something beyond, something to be reached by speech and by dialogue with other speakers. To do this, language cannot be controlled in

---

79. Orwell, *Nineteen Eighty-Four*, 215.
80. Ellul, *Humiliation of the Word*, 128.

advance. How the human can reveal itself in language cannot be predetermined in dialectical speech.

Poetry, novels, philosophies upset the order of thought and transform language so that it expresses new meaning. Such works are Socratic. They have naturally within them the Socratic practice of taking a word, the meaning of which we believe we know, and taking it to the point that it must be recast many times in our mind. No great writer ever leaves language the same. One can no more steal a line of Shakespeare than steal the club of Hercules. The language of the report, the memorandum, the manual, and the media is procedural, actional. In such speech meaning is superseded by function. It is what Anton Zijderveld calls "clichégenic."[81] In participating in e-mail "discussions" everyone is a journalist, typing thoughts and responses just as they come, producing the daily column, the "blog," full of the matter in hand. Any thought can enter into e-mail and, within its limitations, into text messaging. In cyberspace anyone can have a home page, a Web site, a Facebook profile. Everyone is an entry in technique's filing cabinet. Everyone is handling information, the commodity of the technological universe. Everyone is inspecting the merchandise.

TECHNOLOGICAL LEVIATHAN

Technological society is Leviathan. Hobbes is the first to use this term in a secular sense. The frontispiece of the 1651 *Leviathan* has at its top edge a line from the book of Job in the Latin Bible: *Non es potestas Super Terram quae Comparetur ei*. The top half of the frontispiece is a depiction of the "artificial man," a sovereign whose body is composed of tiny drawings of the human populace and who holds in his right hand a sword symbolizing the power of the state and in his left a crosier symbolizing the power of the church.

In the bottom half of the frontispiece are depicted ten analogical scenes of civil and ecclesiastical power, five on the right and five on the left. For example, a scene with banners, muskets, swords, and pikes, the paraphernalia of war, is depicted. Opposite is a scene with pikes on which are written various logical and theological terms. A trident has "syllogis-me" inscribed by syllables on each of its tines. On the two prongs of another pike are written "real" and "intentional." On a larger two-pronged staff is the distinction between "spiritual" and "temporal"; another has "direct" and "indirect" (referring to forms of proof). These are the instruments of ecclesiastical battle or dispute—the tools of Scholastic logic and metaphysics. The bottom frame

81. Zijderveld, *On Clichés*, chap. 2.

opposes a scene of battle among knights, with an army in the background, against a scene of theological disputation or perhaps a court of canon law. War versus words: we are reminded of Hobbes's view that only power, not words, maintains social order.

The line Hobbes quotes from Job is the description the Lord gives of the Leviathan, the subject of chapter 41: "Upon the earth there is not his like." The second line completing the verse is "a creature without fear" (Job 41:33). The forty-first chapter begins with the Lord's asking, "Can you draw out Leviathan with a fishhook, or press down his tongue with a cord?" (Job 41:1). It ends, "He beholds everything that is high; he is king over all the sons of pride" (Job 41:34). Leviathan is king over all proud creatures. There are basically two reasons for the Lord to call attention to Leviathan and to the other great beast, Behemoth (the crocodile and the hippopotamus), but more fully they are mythical beasts involved in a long tradition. *Behemoth* is the title of another of Hobbes's works. The first reason is that man is only one of God's creatures and is not the measure of all things. Leviathan cannot be made to do or be whatever man desires. This is the point of the Lord's series of questions in the first verses of chapter 41. The second reason is that man's suffering is not unique; it must be understood with the total perspective of the cosmos.

Hobbes's *Leviathan* is the book of Job for modern man. It is a book of wisdom for the citizen of the modern state. In his work on the citizen, *De cive*, Hobbes says in his preface to the reader: "In this Book thou shalt finde briefly described the duties of man, First as Men, then as Subjects, Lastly, as Christians."[82] The book of Job is advice on how to live in terms of the absolute power of nature. *Leviathan* is advice on how to live in terms of the absolute power of the state. The Leviathan of nature and the Leviathan of the state are both powers that are blind to the individual. The individual must, by studying the book of Job, learn the art of ancient life and, by studying the book of Hobbes, learn the art of modern life. Hobbes's advice holds true for the technological order that succeeded the order of the modern state as he knew it. Technological order is absolute.

The covenant that man has with God causes man to give up his right to be the measure of all things. The Lord reminds man of this with Leviathan. Hobbes says that every man makes a covenant and gives up his right concerning his self to the commonwealth: "This done, the Multitude so united in one Person, is called a common-wealth, in latine civitas. This is the Generation of that great leviathan, or rather (to speake more reverently) of that *Mortall God*, to which wee owe under the *Immortall God*, our peace

---

82. Hobbes, *De cive*, 29.

and defence."[83] In his discussion of books of the Bible in part 3 of *Leviathan*, Hobbes says that he regards the book of Job as a moral treatise: "concerning a question in ancient time much disputed, *why wicked men have often prospered in this world, and good men have been afflicted.*"[84]

The covenant with Leviathan was made without our knowledge in the twilight of the Renaissance and the dawn of the modern world. Descartes was there. It was a covenant of method: that truth would always be a matter of right reasoning, that nature was a machine. Vaucanson's mechanical figures and duck were there.[85] Condorcet was there, with his confession to using the deceptive art of the Pharisees. John Wyatt was there, with his machine made "in order to spin without fingers." Machines were transformed from a matter of curiosity into a means of production. Once begun, none of this was reversible. Social order followed the machine, and all, including man's identity, had to be rethought: man a machine, the brain a computer.

The computer has become the meaning of technology in the way that the machine originally was what technology meant. As with the machine before, there is now the constant assertion that the computer is just an instrument and that it is at the direction of its users. Ellul says, "The computer is nothing but, and nothing more than, technology. Yet it performs what was virtually the action of the technological whole, it brings it to its bare perfection; it makes it obvious."[86] Neil Postman in *Technopoly* says, "I am constantly amazed how obediently people accept explanations that begin with the words 'The computer shows . . .' or 'The computer has determined . . .' It is Technopoly's equivalent of the sentence 'It is God's will.'"[87] All is united in one Person, the technical man.

Ellul says, "Man's central, his—I might say—metaphysical problem is no longer the existence of God and his own existence in terms of that sacred mystery. The problem is now the conflict between that absolute rationality and what has hitherto constituted his person."[88] The medium of the technological commonwealth is the ensemble of means, the certainty that is achieved in all parts of life without need of wisdom or virtue. Now what do you say? "Can you draw out Leviathan with a fishhook, or press down his tongue with a cord? . . . Upon the earth there is not his like, a creature

83. Hobbes, *Leviathan*, 227.

84. Ibid., 420.

85. On Vaucanson, see Giedion, *Mechanization Takes Command*, 34–46.

86. Ellul, *Technological System*, 74.

87. Postman, *Technopoly*, 115.

88. Ellul, *Technological System*, 74.

without fear. He beholds everything that is high; he is the king over all the sons of pride."

In his modern version of the story of Job, *J. B.: A Play in Verse*, Archibald MacLeish reminds us that Job is also modern man. As J. B. listens, Nickles says that none of us know the truth as Job did; we do not have his cause to know.[89] J. B.'s wife, Sarah, says that we, like Job, can cry for justice, but there is no way to obtain it.[90] Technique holds dominion and it provides only order; it provides nothing transcendent. But it cannot be that technique's dominion is complete. If it were, none of what can be said of its presence could be said. No one would know enough to find anything wrong with it. No one would know enough to listen.

We are thrown back on the old Socratic spirit of the examined life that can be discussed among friends. In his preface to the reader of *De cive* Hobbes says, "But in after times, *Socrates* is said to have been the first, who truly loved this civill Science, although hitherto not thoroughly understood, yet glimmering forth as through a cloud in the government of the Common weale, and that he set so great a value on this, that utterly abandoning, and despising all other parts of Philosophy, he wholly embraced this, as judging it onely worth the labour of his minde."[91]

The problem philosophy and specifically moral philosophy faces is how to keep itself alive in the age of technology—how, that is, to keep questions of self-knowledge, civil wisdom, and virtue alive in an age that has no need of them. If philosophy yields to the technical impulse, it loses its ancient task of pursuing the Socratic ideal of wisdom and the best life. The four cardinal virtues are put aside in favor of the pursuit of moral theories and moral decision procedures that are tied to moral argument that does not touch the problem of human character and its basis in moral memory. If the self is dissolved into to fascination with the person, the ancient quest for self-knowledge is lost and we find ourselves in a world of persons who are less than citizens and who lack all basis for attention to the *summum bonum*.

The moral philosopher must chart a course that only few can follow, and they are those who can see with the mind's eye the sense of the human that has not been absorbed in the mass life of the technical. There is no known method to establish this course. It depends upon our powers of memory to recall what was left behind in the formation of the modern world and to seek a balance between what has gone before in our culture and what is now the order of things. To consider this issue is a call for the

89. MacLeish, *J. B.*, 147.
90. Ibid., 151.
91. Hobbes, *De cive*, 29.

sleeper to awake. And if we do so we can say with Plato, at the end of the *Republic*, we shall fare well.

Bibliography

Aeschylus. *The Seven Against Thebes*. Translated by Herbert Weir Smith. Cambridge: Harvard University Press, 1988.

Aquinas, Thomas. *Commentary on the Nicomachean Ethics*. 2 vols. Translated by C. I. Litzinger. Chicago: Regnery, 1964.

———. *The Disputed Questions on Truth*. 2 vols. Translated by Robert W. Mulligan. Chicago: Regnery, 1953.

Aristophanes. *Acharnians*. Translated by Jeffrey Henderson. Cambridge: Harvard University Press, 1998.

Aristotle. *Aristotle's Nicomachean Ethics*. Translated by Robert C. Bartlett and Susan D. Collins. Chicago: University of Chicago Press, 2011.

———. *The Complete Works of Aristotle*. Edited by Jonathan Barnes. 2 vols. Princeton: Princeton University Press, 1984.

Armin, Robert. *Fools and Jesters: With a Reprint of Robert Armin's Nest of Ninnies*. Edited by J. P. Collier. London: Printed for the Shakespeare Society, 1842.

Augustine. *Confessions*. Translated by F. J. Sheed. Indianapolis: Hackett, 1993.

Bacon, Francis. "Of Vicissitude of Things." In *The Major Works*, edited by Brian Vickers, 451–54. New York: Oxford University Press, 2002.

———. *The Works of Francis Bacon*. 4 vols. Edited by James Spedding, Robert Leslie Ellis, and Douglas Denon Heath. New York: Garrett, 1968.

Benjamin, Walter. "Das Kunstwerk im Zeitalter seiner technischen Reproduzierbarkeit." In *Illuminationen: Ausgewählte Schriften*, edited by Siegfried Unseld, 136–69. Frankfurt: Suhrkamp, 1977.

Berdyaev, Nicolas. *The Fate of Man in the Modern World*. Translated by Donald A. Lowrie. Ann Arbor: University of Michigan Press, 1961.

Berman, Paul. "The Philosopher of Islamic Terror." *New York Times Magazine*, March 23, 2003, 24, 29, 56, 59, 65–67.

Borges, Jorge Luis. "The Immortal." In *Collected Fictions*, translated by Andrew Hurley, 183–95. New York: Penguin, 1998.

Borgmann, Albert. *Technology and the Character of Contemporary Life*. Chicago: University of Chicago Press, 1984.

Borradori, Giovanna. *Philosophy in a Time of Terror: Dialogues with Jürgen Habermas and Jacques Derrida*. Chicago: University of Chicago Press, 2003.

Brant, Sebastian. *Sebastian Brants Narrenschiff*. Edited by Friedrich Zarncke. Hildesheim: Olms, 1961.

———. *The Ship of Fools*. Translated by Edwin H. Zeydel. New York: Dover, 1962.

Burroughs, Augusten. *A Wolf at the Table: A Memoir of My Father.* New York: St. Martin's, 2008.

Butler, Joseph. "Sermons." In *British Moralists*, edited by L. A. Selby-Bigge. Indianapolis: Bobbs-Merrill, 1964.

Cassirer, Ernst. *An Essay on Man: An Introduction to a Philosophy of Human Culture.* New Haven: Yale University Press, 1944.

———. "Form und Technik." In *Symbol, Technik, Sprache: Aufsätze aus den Jahren, 1927–1933*, edited by Ernst Wolfgang Orth and John Michael Krois, 39–91. Hamburg: Meiner, 1985.

———. "The Influence of Language upon the Development of Scientific Thought." *Journal of Philosophy* 39 (1942) 309–27.

———. *The Myth of the State.* New Haven: Yale University Press, 1946.

———. *The Philosophy of Symbolic Forms.* 3 vols. Translated by Ralph Manheim. New Haven: Yale University Press, 1953–57.

———. *The Philosophy of Symbolic Forms.* Vol. 4, *The Metaphysics of Symbolic Forms.* Edited by John Michael Krois and Donald Phillip Verene. Translated by John Michael Krois. New Haven: Yale University Press, 1996.

———. *Symbol, Myth, and Culture: Essays and Lectures of Ernst Cassirer, 1935–1945.* Edited by Donald Phillip Verene. New Haven: Yale University Press, 1979.

Castelli, Enrico. *Il tempo esaurito.* Rome: Bussola, 1947.

Cicero. *Brutus* and *Orator.* Translated by G. L. Hendrickson and H. M. Hubbell. Cambridge: Harvard University Press, 2001.

———. *De officiis.* Translated by Walter Miller. Cambridge: Harvard University Press, 2001.

———. *De partitione oratoria.* Translated by H. Rackham. Cambridge: Harvard University Press, 2004.

———. *Tusculan Disputations.* Translated by J. E. King. Cambridge: Harvard University Press, 2001.

Cleckley, Hervey. *The Mask of Sanity.* 5th ed. Augusta, GA: Emily S. Cleckley, 1988.

Cusanus, Nicholas. *Of Learned Ignorance.* Translated by Germain Heron. London: Routledge & Kegan Paul, 1954.

Dante Alighieri. *The Divine Comedy: Inferno.* Translation and commentary by Charles S. Singleton. Princeton: Princeton University Press, 1970.

Descartes, René. *The Philosophical Writings of Descartes.* Translated by John Cottingham, Robert Stoothoff, and Dugald Murdoch. 3 vols. Cambridge: Cambridge University Press, 1985.

Dewey, John. *Theory of the Moral Life.* New York: Irvington, 1960.

Doran, John. *The History of Court Fools.* New York: Haskell House, 1966.

Dreyfus, Hubert L. *What Computers Still Can't Do: A Critique of Artificial Reason.* Cambridge: MIT Press, 1994.

Ducassé, Pierre. *Histoire des techniques.* Paris: Presses Universitaires de France, 1945.

Eco, Umberto. *Travels in Hyperreality: Essays.* Translated by William Weaver. London: Picador, 1987.

Eliade, Mircea. *The Myth of the Eternal Return: Cosmos and History.* Translated by Willard R. Trask. Princeton: Princeton University Press, 2005.

Eliot, T. S. "The Hollow Men." In *Selected Poems.* New York: Harcourt, Brace, 1964.

Ellul, Jacques. *The Humiliation of the Word.* Translated by Joyce Main Hanks. Grand Rapids: Eerdmans, 1985.

———. *The Political Illusion.* Translated by Konrad Kellen. New York: Knopf, 1967.

———. *Propaganda: The Formation of Men's Attitudes.* Translated by Konrad Kellen and Jean Lerner. New York: Knopf, 1965.

———. *The Technological Bluff.* Translated by Geoffrey W. Bromiley. Grand Rapids: Eerdmans, 1990.

———. *The Technological Society.* Translated by John Wilkinson. New York: Knopf, 1964.

———. *The Technological System.* Translated by Joachim Neugroschel. New York: Continuum, 1980.

Erasmus, Desiderius. *The Praise of Folly.* Translated by Clarence H. Miller. New Haven: Yale University Press, 1979.

Faulkner, William, *Requiem for a Nun.* New York: Vintage, 2012.

Findlay, John N. *Hegel: A Re-examination.* London: Allen & Unwin, 1958.

Floorman, Samuel C. *The Existential Pleasures of Engineering.* New York: St. Martin's, 1976.

Frost, Robert. "The Road Not Taken." In *Modern Poems*, edited by Richard Ellmann and Robert O'Clair, New York: Norton, 1976.

Gann, David. "The Chameleon: The Many Lives of Frédéric Bourdin." *The New Yorker*, August 11 and 18, 2008, 66–79.

Giedion, Siegfried. *Mechanization Takes Command: A Contribution to Anonymous History.* Oxford: Oxford University Press, 1948.

Graubard, Stephen, editor. *The Artificial Intelligence Debate: False Starts, Real Foundations.* Cambridge: MIT Press, 1988.

Guicciardini, Francesco. *Ricordi.* Milan: Rizzoli, 1977.

Hare, Robert D. *Without Conscience: The Disturbing World of the Psychopaths among Us.* New York: Guilford, 1993.

Hegel, G. W. F. *Elements of the Philosophy of Right.* Edited by Allen W. Wood. Translated by N. B. Nisbet. Cambridge: Cambridge University Press, 1991.

———. *Hegel's Science of Logic.* Translated by A. V. Miller. London: Allen & Unwin, 1969.

———. *Phenomenology of Spirit.* Translated by A. V. Miller. Oxford: Clarendon, 1977.

Heidegger, Martin. *The Question Concerning Technology and Other Essays.* Translated by William Lovitt. New York: Harper & Row, 1977.

Heraclitus. "Heraclitus of Ephesus." In G. S. Kirk and J. E. Raven, *The Presocratic Philosophers: A Critical History with a Selection of Texts*, 181–212. Cambridge: Cambridge University Press, 1960.

Herodotus. *The Persian Wars.* Translated by A. D. Godley. Vol. 1. Cambridge: Harvard University Press, 2004.

Hippocrates. "The Oath." In vol. 1 of *Hippocrates.* Translated by W. H. S. Jones. Cambridge: Harvard University Press, 2001.

Hobbes, Thomas. *De cive: The English Edition.* Edited by Howard Warrender. Oxford: Clarendon, 1983.

———. *Leviathan*, edited by C. B. Macpherson. New York: Penguin, 1979.

Homer. *Iliad.* Translated by A. T. Murray, revised by William F. Watt. 2 vols. Cambridge: Harvard University Press, 1999.

Horace. *Ars poetica.* Translated by J. Rushton Fairclough. Cambridge: Harvard University Press, 1999.

Huxley, Aldous. *Ends and Means.* New York: Harper, 1937.

Ihde, Don. *Technology and the Life-World: From Garden to Earth.* Bloomington: University of Indiana Press, 1990.

Ionesco, Eugene. *Rhinoceros and Other Plays.* Translated by Derek Prouse. New York: Grove, 1960.

James, William. *The Letters of William James.* Edited by Henry James. Vol. 1. Boston: Atlantic Monthly, 1920.

Jaspers, Karl. *The Future of Mankind.* Translated by E. B. Ashton. Chicago: University of Chicago Press, 1951.

————. *Man in the Modern Age.* Translated by Eden Paul and Cedar Paul. New York: Doubleday Anchor, 1957.

Jonas, Hans. *The Imperative of Responsibility: In Search of an Ethics for the Technological Age.* Translated by Hans Jonas and David Herr. Chicago: University of Chicago Press, 1984.

Joyce, James. *Finnegans Wake.* Edited by Danis Rose and John O'Hanlon. Cornwall, UK: Houyhuhnm, 2010.

————. *Ulysses.* Edited by Hans Walter Gabler. New York: Vintage, 1993.

Jung, Carl. *Two Essays on Analytical Psychology.* Translated by R. F. C. Hull. New York: Meridian, 1991.

Jűnger, Friedrich Georg. *The Failure of Technology.* Chicago: Regnery, 1949.

Justinian. *Digest.* Translated by Alan Watson. Vol. 1. Philadelphia: University of Pennsylvania Press, 1985.

————. *Institutes.* Translated by Peter Birks and Grant McLeod, with the Latin text of Paul Krueger. Ithaca: Cornell University Press, 1987.

Kant, Immanuel. *Critique of Judgement.* Translated by J. C. Meredith. Oxford: Clarendon, 1964.

————. *Foundations of the Metaphysics of Morals.* Translated by Lewis White Beck. Indianapolis: Bobbs-Merrill, 1959.

La Mettrie, Julien Offray de. *Man a Machine.* Translated by Richard A. Watson and Maya Rybalka. Indianapolis: Hackett, 1994.

Levi, Albert William. *The High Road of Humanity: The Seven Ethical Ages of Western Man.* Edited by Donald Phillip Verene and Molly Black Verene. Amsterdam: Rodopi, 1995.

Lévi-Strauss, Claude. *The Raw and the Cooked: Introduction to a Science of Mythology.* Translated by John Weightman and Doreen Weightman. New York: Harper, 1969.

Lewis, Bernard. *The Crisis in Islam.* New York: Modern, 2003.

————. *What Went Wrong: Western Impact and Middle Eastern Response.* New York: Oxford University Press, 2002.

Longinus. *On the Sublime.* Translated by Donald Russell. Cambridge: Harvard University Press, 1995.

MacIntyre, Alasdair. "Does Applied Ethics Rest on a Mistake?" *The Monist* 67 (1984) 498–513.

MacLeish, Archibald. *J. B.: A Play in Verse.* Boston: Houghton Mifflin, 1956.

Marcuse, Herbert. *One-Dimensional Man: Studies in the Ideology of Advanced Industrial Society.* Boston: Beacon, 1964.

Marx, Karl. *Capital.* Vol. 1. Moscow: Foreign Language Publishing House, 1954.

McLuhan, Marshall. *Understanding Media: The Extensions of Man.* 2nd ed. New York: Signet, 1966.

Mill, John Stuart. *Utilitarianism.* New York: Liberal Arts, 1957.

Miller, Henry. *The World of Sex and the White Phagocytes.* London: Calder & Boyars, 1970.

Mumford, Lewis. *Technics and Civilization.* New York: Harcourt, Brace, 1934.

Novak, Maximillian E. "The Wild Man Comes to Tea." In *The Wild Man Within: An Image in Western Thought from the Renaissance to Romanticism,* edited by Edward Dudley and Maximillian E. Novak, 183–221. Pittsburgh: Pittsburgh University Press, 1972.

Orwell, George. *Nineteen Eighty-Four: A Novel.* New York: Harcourt, Brace, 1949.

Otto, Rudolph. *The Idea of the Holy.* Oxford: Oxford University Press, 1923. Rev. ed., 1929.

Pascal, Blaise. *Pensées.* Translated by H. F. Stewart. New York: Pantheon, 1950.

Peirce, C. S. "The Fixation of Belief." In *Philosophical Writings of Peirce,* edited by Justus Buchler, 5–22. New York: Dover, 1955.

Pico della Mirandola, Giovanni. "Oration on the Dignity of Man." Translated by Elizabeth Livermore Forbes. In *The Renaissance Philosophy of Man,* edited by Ernst Cassirer et al., 223–54. Chicago: University of Chicago Press, 1956.

Plato. *Complete Works.* Edited by John M. Cooper. Indianapolis: Hackett, 1997.

Plutarch. "Die Pythiae Oraculis." Translated by Frank Cole Babbitt. In vol. 5 of *Moralia.* Cambridge: Harvard University Press, 2003.

Porter, Katherine Anne. *Ship of Fools.* Boston: Little, Brown, 1945.

Postman, Neil. *Technopoly: The Surrender of Culture to Technology.* New York: Random House, 1993.

Pound, Ezra. *The Cantos of Ezra Pound.* New York: New Directions, 1991.

Prichard, H. A. "Does Moral Philosophy Rest on a Mistake?" *Mind* 21 (1912) 21–37.

Quintilian. *Institutio oratoria.* Translated by Donald A. Russell. Cambridge: Harvard University Press, 2001.

Rapp, Friedrich. *Analytical Philosophy of Technology.* Translated by Stanley Carpenter and Theodor Langenbruch. Boston: Reidel, 1981.

Rorty, Richard. *Philosophy and the Mirror of Nature.* Princeton: Princeton University Press, 1979.

Rothenberg, David. *Hand's End: Technology and the Limits of Nature.* Berkeley: University of California Press, 1993.

Rousseau, Jean-Jacques. *The First and Second Discourses.* Translated by Roger D. Masters and Judith R. Masters. New York: St. Martin's, 1964.

Sade, Comte Donatien Alphonse François de. *The Complete Justine, Philosophy in the Bedroom and Other Writings.* Translated by Richard Seaver and Austryn Wainshouse. New York: Grove, 1965.

Seabrook, John. "Suffering Souls: The Search for the Roots of Psychopathy." *The New Yorker,* November 10, 2008, 64–73.

Shaftesbury, Anthony Ashley Cooper, Earl of. *The Life, Unpublished Letters, and Philosophical Regimen of Anthony, Earl of Shaftesbury.* Edited by Benjamin Rand. London: Swann Sonnenschein, 1900.

———. *Second Characters, or the Language of Forms.* Edited by Benjamin Rand. Cambridge: Cambridge University Press, 1914.

Spinoza, Benedict de. *Chief Works.* 2 vols. Translated by R. H. M. Elwes. New York: Dover, 1951.

Stout, Martha. *The Sociopath Next Door: The Ruthless Versus the Rest of Us.* New York: Broadway, 2005.

Bibliography

Swift, Jonathan. *The Writings of Jonathan Swift*. Edited by Robert A. Greenberg and William Bowman Piper. New York: Norton, 1973.

Tao Te Ching. Translated by Stephen Addiss and Stanley Lombardo. Indianapolis: Hackett, 1993.

Thomas, Dylan. "Fern Hill." In *The Poems of Dylan Thomas*, edited by Daniel Jones. New York: New Directions, 1971.

Toffler, Alvin. *Future Shock*. New York: Bantam, 1970.

Ungaretti, Giuseppe. *Vite d'un uomo: Saggi e interventi*. Milan: Mondadori, 1974.

Vico, Giambattista. *The Most Ancient Wisdom of the Italians*. Translated by L. M. Palmer. Ithaca: Cornell University Press, 1988.

———. *The New Science of Giambattista Vico*. Translated by Thomas Goddard Bergin and Max Harold Fisch. Ithaca: Cornell University Press, 1984.

———. *On the Study Methods of Our Time*. Translated by Elio Gianturco. Ithaca: Cornell University Press, 1990.

Vives, Juan Luis. "A Fable about Man." Translated by Nancy Lenkeith. In *The Renaissance Philosophy of Man*, edited by Ernst Cassirer et al., 387–93. Chicago: University of Chicago Press, 1956.

Ward, James Sheridan, et al. *Asylum Light: Stories from the Dr. George A. Zeller Era and Beyond; Peoria State Hospital, Galesburg Mental Health Center, and George A. Zeller Mental Health Center*. Springfield, IL: Mental Health Historic Preservation Society of Central Illinois, 2004.

Whitehead, Alfred North. *Process and Reality: An Essay in Cosmology*. New York: Macmillan, 1929.

Winner, Langdon. *The Whale and the Reactor: A Search for Limits in an Age of High Technology*. Chicago: University of Chicago Press, 1986.

Zeydel, Edwin H. *Sebastian Brant*. New York: Twayne, 1967.

Zijderveld, Anton C. *On Clichés: The Supersedure of Meaning by Function in Modernity*. London: Routledge & Kegan Paul, 1979.

———. *Reality in a Looking-Glass: Rationality through an Analysis of Traditional Folly*. London: Routledge & Kegan Paul, 1982.

Index